STORIES OF GRIT, GRACE, AND THE STRENGTH WE DIDN'T KNOW WE HAD

WHAT SURVIVES THE STORM

COMPILED BY KYRA SCHAEFER

ISBN: 978-1-969615-06-1

Published by As You Wish Publishing
www.asyouwishpublishing.com
connect@asyouwishpublishing.com

Contents

Foreword

By Kyra Schaefer

There are moments in life that ask more of us than we ever thought we could give. Moments that stretch us. Quiet us. Break open something we didn't know was still tender. Moments that don't just pass through us, but reshape us.

This book, *What Survives the Storm*, is a collection of those moments.

Each story within these pages carries something deeply human. Grit, grace, heartbreak, resilience, and the quiet strength that often goes unseen until it's needed most. These are not polished stories meant to impress. They are lived experiences, offered with honesty, courage, and a willingness to be seen.

And that matters so much.

Because when someone chooses to share their truth, especially the parts that were hard to hold, they create a bridge. A place where someone else can recognize themselves and feel a little less alone. That is a genuine gift.

What runs through every story in this book is a quiet willingness to turn inward, to listen, and to share what was found there. These aren't just stories on a page. They are reflections of what it means to be human, to endure, and to keep choosing to stay open, even after life has asked us to close.

As you move through these pages, I hope you find pieces of yourself in unexpected places. A sentence that lingers. A moment that feels familiar. A perspective that gently shifts something inside you.

That is the quiet power of shared truth.

There is no single way to move through a storm. But there is something truly profound about witnessing how others have done it. Not perfectly. Not all at once. But in real, human ways that remind us of what is possible.

This book is not here to tell you who to be or how to heal. It simply offers you something real to sit with.

And sometimes, that is exactly what we need.

A Note from Me to the Authors

To each of you who said yes to being part of this book,

I want you to know how much I see you. Truly.

Sharing your story is not a small thing. It asks for honesty, vulnerability, and a kind of courage that doesn't always get acknowledged. You chose to put something real on the page, something lived, something felt, and that matters more than you may ever fully realize.

Your words carry real weight.

They carry insight, wisdom, and lived experience that someone, somewhere, will need at exactly the right moment. You may never meet the person your story reaches. You may never hear how it helped them take a breath, feel understood, or find their footing again.

But it will. I truly believe that.

Because truth has a way of traveling farther than we can see.

You are so appreciated for your willingness to show up in this way. You are respected for the life that shaped the words you've written. And you are valued, not just for what you created here, but for who you are as a person.

You are loved.

Not for being perfect. Not for having everything figured out. But for your presence, your perspective, and your willingness to contribute something meaningful to this world.

Thank you for trusting this space. Thank you for trusting your voice. And thank you for adding your piece to something that will continue to ripple outward in ways we may never fully know.

With so much gratitude and love,
Kyra

We created a special song just for this book. Listen here: https://tinyurl.com/whatsurvivesthestormsong

If you are interested in contributing to a future collaboration book with As You Wish Publishing, visit us at www.asyouwishpublishing.com/wewrite

CHAPTER

Listening Within: Trusting My Inner Knowing

By Ann Aristides

Ann Aristides

Ann Aristides is an intuitive practitioner whose work bridges analytical insight and energetic awareness. A graduate of the University of St. Thomas, she earned dual degrees in Economics and Spanish, grounding her early academic path in structure and systems thinking.

Her journey later expanded into the study of energy, intuition, and integrative healing, where she received a Master's of Intuition Medicine® from the Academy of Intuition Medicine®. Through this training, Ann developed a refined understanding of the body's energetic systems and their connection to physical and emotional well-being.

Blending intellectual curiosity with intuitive depth, Ann supports others in reconnecting with their inner guidance, strengthening awareness, and cultivating embodied clarity. She lives and practices in the San Francisco Bay Area, where she continues her work at the intersection of intuition, energy, and personal transformation.

Reach Ann via email: annaristides@gmail.com

Chapter 1

Listening Within: Trusting My Inner Knowing

By Ann Aristides

When your mind is calmed, you are able to sit and be. When I was finally able to think in a clear space, with reflection's ability at its peak, I understood the dismissed emotions, aches, and infections from childhood were showing themselves in my adult life as autoimmune diseases. It would seem that I do not take care of my physical body, but this could not be further from reality. As a celiac for over 20 years, I was working out, playing tennis, and eating a healthy diet. Yet, I knew something else was wrong. The doctors told me I was tired because I had young children, the blackouts when I stood were from my gluten-free diet, and the tremors were from anxiety. I was too young to have any serious illness. My instincts told me the system was just being dismissive. My childhood on repeat, but by renowned doctors, not my unconcerned mother.

I was the youngest child in my family, and my mother was not interested in seeking answers for my childhood health issues. Forty-seven years of medical dismissal by people who were supposed to protect, listen, and heal me did not make me question my intuition. I knew something was wrong, but I couldn't see myself clearly enough, energetically, to understand it.

Exhaustion is not a reason for an MRI, in the defense of the system. I raised an issue of concern to my gastroenterologist, who was treating me for celiac disease. I told her that my left leg seemed sluggish. The next day, to my surprise, I received a call from the Multiple Sclerosis clinic at her affiliated hospital. Of course, consistent with my story, that doctor was dismissive and agreed only to give me an MRI because the referring doctor was a friend. Unfortunately, I do have Multiple Sclerosis. I finally had an explanation for my symptoms, and it is likely that I have had Multiple Sclerosis since my teens.

A brilliant quote from Aristotle states, "Knowing yourself is the beginning of all wisdom." We spend the most time throughout our lives with ourselves, not our spouse, children, partner, or friends. Yet, most people take the least amount of time to really look within. We are taught to learn and care for others, or to only "think" of ourselves, but not in ways that truly benefit the mind, body, and spirit as a whole. Spirit, in my use, is defined as our inner sense of being. Our sense of self shapes who we end up as in life. Our sense of self is determined in our spirit and in our genes, body, mind, and energy. Knowing your spirit is the key to knowing oneself.

In our modern world, we are most often taught to override our naturally integrated awareness. Instead of trusting intuition, we are conditioned to rely on what we are told we should think, choose, or pursue. We are all born with implicit memories we need for survival, which we call instincts. Instincts are fast, integrated, and informed by far more data than conscious thought can process at any given moment. As we age, our thoughts can take over these instincts, guiding us to what might not be the ideal reaction or perspective. We learn to trust external voices over our own internal knowing. Conscious thoughts are the last step in the chain of perception, yet we are trained to use our conscious thoughts as our guide. When clarity is already present, overthinking only creates unnecessary complexity. This leads to disappointment, anxiety, and self-doubt. When we stop overriding ourselves, we stop fighting reality. And from that place, decision-making becomes simpler, steadier, and far more powerful.

The more I listened to my spirit, the more my intuition strengthened. Although knowing my spirit and myself has been a lengthy and variable process. Reading and seeing others seems to be much easier and clearer to me. My biggest challenge is seeing and healing myself in partnership with my spirit. Sitting in silence with yourself in meditation is a challenge within. To be a neutral and impartial witness to your own spirit can be beautiful. Feeling a sense of lightness while being grounded is euphoric. Your mind lets go of the chatter. In early meditations, I felt a sense of inner peace that I had longed for, and I didn't really know how much I needed it. This was my very first step in beginning to know myself, focusing inward, and starting to take charge of my mind.

I immersed myself in learning the complex architecture of the energetic body and its impact on physical health. That knowledge now works in partnership with my spirit, enabling me to facilitate energetic healing while expanding my intuitive capacity beyond what I once believed possible. The information clarified why it is difficult to energetically see myself without bias and intellect. My knowledge and experiences in life have clouded my clarity by overriding my spirit when I am looking at myself with conscious thoughts and facts.

While learning, I experienced my first personal energetic healing during an intense guided meditation to shift energy. A fibroadenoma that had been in my right breast for 15 years disappeared when an intense energy vibrated through my physical body, creating a shift and release. I understand that this needed to happen to have a mindset open to all things, to all possibilities, to all I was going to learn and feel. I had wanted to believe, but my analytical mind had been the primary source of my knowledge and understanding of information. I experienced something that was tangible, yet not explainable, in the Western medical curriculum. I experienced the benefit from a cellular healing energy that transcended space and time. The intense energy released an attachment from my physical body and my energetic body. This form of healing released my first noticeable block, and it happened before I was genuinely accepting of medical energy healing. This was the transcendent experience I needed to begin to know myself on a higher level.

My Multiple Sclerosis diagnosis was an empowering relief. My gluten-free diet, Pilates, and being active were helping my physical body, but my energetic body needed to be cleared of past patterns. My spirit has guided me with resilience and empowered me with strength, and has given me the confidence to not let my health issues define me, but fuel me. I was never allowed to be ill as a child, and maybe this is one of the biggest and most unexpected blessings I was given as an adult. I don't want my illnesses to define me, as they are woven into my daily life like breakfast, lunch, and dinner. I listen to my body when it needs to rest, and I give it grace for all that it has brought me.

Energetic healing is rooted in the imbalance of our energetic bodies, which hold unseen layers of our thoughts, emotions, traumas, and relationships before they manifest physically. Knowing oneself and one's own energetic spirit helps to reveal and acknowledge these imbalances. Our physical and energetic spirit carries an inner intelligence that communicates to us, but I have had to learn not to override it with dismissive thoughts and actions. I listen to my signals, and this awareness has brought me strength and wisdom. Energetic healing is less about fixing and more about balance and occurs naturally when we have the courage to know ourselves and our spirit. I have learned to treat my energetic spirit as well as I have treated my physical body, and have compassion for both when they need to slow down.

My body and spirit have guided me to energetic and intuitive healing, opening my awareness to new and deeper ways of knowing myself. I know that my health has given me the opportunity to begin to learn this work, and I feel a profound sense of gratitude for it. I had never thought of my spirit in the way I see it today, as it is powerful, loyal, intelligent, communicative, and creative. It has given me a perspective on life that I did not have before. I would not have chosen Multiple Sclerosis, but I am grateful it has led me towards the path of greater connection to my spirit, bringing me more compassion, awareness, and curiosity for myself.

My personal growth through meditation, intuition, and being open to additional ways of healing has been life-changing. My intuition has been heightened, revealing depths within myself I did not know I could access. I am still getting to know myself, and I will be pursuing a stronger bond with my spirit for the rest of my life. Healing from Multiple Sclerosis is a journey I will continue to walk with patience and commitment. I will continue to work with Western medical doctors to help find a cure for Multiple Sclerosis, while also working with other energy healers and my own inner practice to heal myself.

CHAPTER

Let It Go
A Journey of Trust and Grace
By M. Bennett

M. Bennett

M. Bennett lives on California's Central Coast, where she and her husband tend a small farm with chickens, dogs, and cats. A mother of three compassionate adult children, she draws inspiration from family, animals, and the quiet rhythms of rural life. Her writing explores resilience, humor, and the extraordinary hidden in ordinary moments. When she's not writing, she's caring for her farm, observing life's small miracles, and reflecting on the stories that connect us all. Learn more at www.harmonyhouseranch.com.

Chapter 2

Let It Go: A Journey of Trust and Grace

By M. Bennett

My brother called me out of the blue. The moment his name lit up my phone, I paused mid-step in the kitchen. He rarely called unless he needed something, and even then, it was usually a two-sentence conversation, sharp as a tap on the shoulder. I answered anyway, wiping my hands on a dish towel, bracing myself.

He didn't bother with a greeting.

"You need to move back home and take care of Mom," he said, his voice clipped, as if he were delivering a verdict.

I swallowed hard. "I have three kids and a job," I reminded him, keeping my tone calm. It felt strange having to defend my life to my own brother, but that had been our dynamic for decades. Out of the three of us, I was the only one raising children. He and his wife didn't want kids because, as he often put it, they didn't want to 'give up their freedom.' My sister, the youngest of the three of us, had never married and lived about 200 miles from Mom.

Meanwhile, I was living three thousand miles away, working full-time at a high school, running a household, raising three children, tending to pets, and doing my best to keep our heads above water. My mother and siblings lived in their familiar East Coast orbit, while I lived on the opposite side of the country, in a life shaped very differently from theirs. My father, my steady, grounding presence, had died ten years earlier. Without him, the subtle gaps in our relationships had widened into canyons.

"Then you need to help pay to get her into an assisted living apartment," he snapped, irritation crackling through the line.

"With what money?" I asked.

He didn't know, had never asked, how hard things had been. My husband had been unemployed for three years, and those years had hollowed us out financially. Even after he finally found a new job, the debt clung to us like a shadow we couldn't shake. If I left work, even temporarily, we would lose everything. That was how razor-thin our margin was.

Before I could explain, before I could gather my breath, a voice rang through me; clear, firm, unmistakably wise:

He's made up his mind. He won't listen to anything you say.

It cut through the air like a bell tone. I froze, the phone pressed against my ear, the familiar kitchen around me suddenly still. The kids were in their rooms doing homework, their pencils scratching faintly from down the hall. My husband was working quietly in the family room, the soft hum of his computer a steady backdrop. The whole house felt calm, except for the storm pouring from the other end of the phone.

My mouth closed. I heard my brother's anger, his assumptions, his accusations, but I said nothing. That inner voice had spoken so clearly, I trusted it with absolute certainty. So I let the storm of vitriolic words pass through me like wind through an open window. And then I let them go.

Later that night, when the house had settled into its evening rhythm, old memories floated up like silt stirred from the bottom of a river. Childhood patterns I thought I'd outgrown resurfaced with sharp clarity.

My brother had always been the one who skirted rules, doing whatever he pleased; loudly, recklessly, with no thought for the aftermath. My mother eventually stopped asking him to do his chores and turned to me instead. So I took them on. I did my chores, his chores, sometimes my sister's, slipping into the role of helper without protest.

When I went out to buy Mom a birthday gift, my brother would ask me to pick up one for him, too. When I made plans with friends, Mom would ask me to take my sister because she didn't want her to feel left out. My sister borrowed my clothes regularly; if she particularly liked something, she would fold it neatly into her own drawers, as if it had always been hers.

My brother was, and still is, ruthless in his teasing, inventing demeaning names and hurling them with the precision of someone who took pleasure in the impact. I became a reliable target.

And every single time, even long before adulthood taught me the language for it, I let it go.

The next day, my mother called and asked me the very question my brother had demanded. Her voice was softer, hesitant, as if she were repeating something she didn't fully agree with.

I knew instantly he had put her up to it.

"Mom," I said gently, "you know I have the kids. You know I have to work. You know I can't afford to take time off. But you are always welcome to live with us." Mom knew our situation.

I had made that offer many times. Each time she replied, "Everyone I know is here. I don't know anyone there."

I understood. The familiar is a powerful anchor.

Still, a quiet ache rose:

Why must I always be the one who bends?

And once again, I let it go.

Months passed. When Thanksgiving came, I called and left a message. Then again, at Christmas. More messages. Her silence wasn't unusual; she was never good at returning calls, but a worry began tapping at me. I told myself that if anything were wrong, my brother would call.

But life swept us up in a tide of responsibilities. My mother-in-law had been in and out of the hospital. My father-in-law's Alzheimer's was accelerating. He was an active force, always on the go. Alzheimer's had not changed that. I said to my husband, "Your grandmother must have been a saint! He's a handful!" We were constantly driving over to check on them, removing car keys after minor accidents, discovering spare keys, locking steering wheels, finding more spare keys, and rerouting their phone calls to ours because scammers had drained thousands of dollars from their accounts. We were both running on fumes.

Six days after the new year, I opened my email and found a short, curt message from my brother:

Mom had died two days earlier.

I sat there staring at the screen, stunned. My breath wouldn't come. The room seemed to tilt slightly, as if I had stepped onto a rocking boat.

Why hadn't he told me she was ill? Why hadn't he called?

When I asked, his response was cold, sharp enough to cut:

"You could have called."

He had no idea what we had been dealing with. He didn't ask. He assumed. He judged. And once again, that voice, steady and precise, rose inside me:

He doesn't care. He won't listen to anything you say.

It felt like truth delivered straight from the source; undeniable, crisp, free of emotion. A spiritual instinct. A protective whisper from G.U.S. (God, universe, spirit) guiding me to step back and release the weight I'd carried for so long. Once again, a storm of words, nasty and brutish, washed over me. And once again, I let them go.

I realized then that every time that voice had spoken, I had trusted it immediately. It didn't feel like a thought. It felt like guidance; clean, clear, purposeful. As if something wiser than me was pointing me toward peace and away from ancient wounds.

Did my brother's words hurt? Yes.

Do they still hurt sometimes? Yes.

Will I ever reconcile it? No.

And somehow, knowing that felt like its own kind of resolution.

Some things are not meant to be untangled.

Some people are not meant to understand you.

Some battles are not ours to fight, because they never belonged to us in the first place.

So I release the roles assigned to me long ago.

I release the burden of being the flexible one, the responsible one, the catch-all for what others refused to carry.

I release the urge to explain myself to people committed to misunderstanding me.

I let it go.

And I let G.U.S. handle the rest.

CHAPTER

Who Ya Gonna Call?

Stacy Christopher

Stacy Marie Christopher (she/her) is an ordained minister, Reiki Master and licensed therapist. It has been her absolute honor to study with the Reverend Doctor Michael Beckwith, globally beloved psychic medium Tony Stockwell, "Psychic Sergeant" Peter Close, renowned animal communicator Elizabeth Ayer Lee and award-winning podcast creator Ann Theato. Stacy loves working with open-minded, creative liberals on their journey to increase motivation and direction via aligning with their inner guidance. Her passions include advocating for justice and equality, volunteering in animal rescue, and being a massive theater nerd. A portion of all proceeds from her individual book sales go to Planned Parenthood and The Trevor Project.

Website: TheBloomingMystic.com
FB/IG/Threads: The Blooming Mystic

Chapter 3

Who Ya Gonna Call?

By Stacy Christopher

After two grueling hours in holiday-weekend traffic, my bladder and I were thrilled to finally arrive at the hotel. But then I realized, to my horror, the car fob wasn't in the pocket where I always kept it. Thinking it must have slipped out along the way, I checked the seat, and then everywhere I could reach, with increasing agitation. It dawned on me that if I turned the car off, I couldn't turn it on again. My only option was to drive all the way back home and search the area around my parking space. Groaning, I steeled myself to ask the valet to watch my car so I could hobble inside and visit the restroom.

Before I finish this story, please allow me to digress. Earlier that day, I was in a Zoom class on psychic development. I was delighted that my breakout-room partner was Eddie, whose quirky nonconformity played nicely with my own. Straightaway, he said he sensed that I was as stubborn as a truckload of mules and hated asking for help, then suggested I call on my ancestors for assistance since "people-ing" wasn't my strong suit. Unsure how to react to this epic truth-bomb, I admitted that I didn't know anything about my ancestors, having grown up in an oppressive miasma of family secrets.

"Doesn't matter," he said. "They know you, and they don't give a toss about that old nonsense where they are now."

Having knocked the wind out of me, he cheerily launched into a guided meditation to "plant in my stony heart a seed of willingness" to ask for and accept guidance. Coming from anyone else, this would have annoyed me no end, possibly prompting me to "accidentally" lose my internet connection, but I had a soft spot for Eddie's matchless insouciance. I thanked him and said I'd hop right on it, then proceeded to put it out of my mind entirely in a flurry of last-minute packing.

Sitting in traffic on the way to the hotel, though, I pondered the etheric doorway that had been opened. It reminded me of a story called *The Hymn of the Pearl* I'd learned years ago in a class on Gnosticism. It felt like a real game-changer at the time, but, as with so many things, I tucked it away rather than applying it to my life with any vigor or regularity.

Here's the CliffsNotes version of the tale as I remember it: Once upon a time, the divine son of divine beings was given a mission to incarnate on the earth plane, search the world for a glorious pearl, and return home with it. Our unnamed hero agreed and left home filled with optimism. Once embodied, he took full advantage of his new physicality, enthusiastically engaging in all the delights the world had to offer. Eventually, though, he began to lose the plot. He trusted the wrong people. He indulged and over-indulged. Days and nights began to merge until he couldn't recall why he'd chosen to incarnate in the first place. Finally, in deep despair, he cried out to his parents that he needed their help because somehow it had all gone terribly wrong. (It's a very relatable story.)

A messenger instantly arrived to remind him of his true origin and his quest. Reinvigorated, he rose from his misery with pep in his step and searched for the pearl, only to find it was guarded by a massive dragon. He drew his sword but realized that it was insufficient for dragon slaying. Suddenly, he was inspired to sing to the mighty creature. His voice trembled, and his words failed him, so he sang his own name, and the names of his parents. His voice got stronger, and he proclaimed himself a divine being temporarily housed in human form, with a goal to achieve. Enchanted by his song, the dragon fell asleep so that our hero could take the pearl and return home with it.

Such lofty thoughts, however, were nowhere to be found as I prepared to exit my still-running car and approach the valet. My mind was swimming, as were my back teeth, so I made things even worse by beating myself up. Why hadn't I checked my pocket for the fob before leaving? How could I have been such a dimwit? Did I have enough gas to get back home? Could I gas up without cutting the engine since I couldn't restart it? Would I flip out entirely and cause things to devolve into a "film at 11" situation? I had no dignity left to gather as I opened the car door and got out with a grunt. Lo and behold, the fob was sitting on top of the car!

You might well ask how it could possibly have stayed there during two hours of driving on highways and surface streets. Why didn't anyone notice it and honk to get my attention or even point and laugh while idling next to me on the 405? I don't know. It didn't make any sense then, and it still doesn't. The fob itself isn't magnetic.

Calling out to those in spirit is extremely magnetic, though, especially when we've tried our best and taken every action available to us. I routinely call on my loved ones to assist with everyday challenges, choosing whose help to seek based on the task. When newly-arrived animals at the shelter are terrified of human touch, I ask my dogs to comfort them in ways that I can't. When I'm baffled and need help understanding or organizing anything, I ask my mother to help me make sense of it all. When I'm speaking to a group or writing something (like this), I ask The Rev, one of my dear mentors, to help me communicate clearly and effectively, with a pinch of pizzazz.

Establishing contact with my ancestors, though, has unlocked a whole new level of awareness for me. I hope it does the same for you, friend. When the news reports go from bad to worse to horrific on any given day, I know now that I can lean on my ancestors. They endured wars, famines, dictators and every sort of injustice and oppression. When I feel overwhelmed and useless, I ask to be shown some useful action I can take right now, right where I am. When I receive a clear answer, I act on their guidance, even when my voice trembles and my steps falter and the tools I possess seem wildly insufficient. And then I entrust them with the bigger picture, since their wisdom and influence are vastly greater than my own. Ask, receive, act, trust. Repeat as needed, all day, every day.

I didn't choose to incarnate at this particular time just to be a passive doom-scroller, although it's very easy for me to fall into that trap. I came to serve the greater good, which requires taking action. After all, that fob didn't just magically appear as I sat lamenting its absence; I literally had to get off my butt in order to see it. I couldn't claim the pearl until I faced the dragon and started singing.

Now, here's the final (and possibly my favorite) detail: as I lurched gracelessly from the car, the song "Ghostbusters" was playing full blast on someone's radio. And just as I saw the fob, I heard "Who Ya Gonna Call?" A voice in my head called out enthusiastically, "An-cestors!" I may not have known anything about my ancestors, but they clearly know that I can't resist a corny musical moment.

Your ancestors know you, too, because you're the culmination of all their hopes and dreams. They are waiting to help you remember that you're a spiritual being having a human experience, to celebrate with you and to mourn with you, and to guide you in living the life you chose before you incarnated this time around. When the day of reunion eventually comes, imagine the exquisite pearl you'll be bringing back with you to your etheric welcome home party! I'm sure the DJ will have "Ghostbusters" on their playlist.

(And, Eddie, since my arms can't reach all the way across the pond, I'm asking my ancestors to give you a hug from me. Thanks, mate.)

CHAPTER *Four*

Epiphany on the 101

Karen Gabler

Karen Gabler

Karen Gabler is an intuitive mentor, psychic medium, animal communicator, healer and Reiki master. She is also a best-selling author, teacher and inspirational speaker, as well as an award-winning attorney. Karen is passionate about encouraging others to find their highest purpose and live their best lives. She facilitates intuitive connections with her clients' guides and loved ones in spirit and mentors her clients through personal and business issues, combining her practical legal and business experience with her innate intuitive ability to receive guidance from higher sources.

Karen is a recurring guest on spiritual podcasts, conducting readings and answering spiritual questions. She also presents workshops and seminars on a variety of business, spiritual and personal development topics. Karen earned a Bachelor of Arts in psychology from the University of Hawaii and a Juris Doctorate from the William S. Richardson School of Law at the University of Hawaii. She has pursued wide-ranging education in interpersonal development and the spiritual sciences and has completed the Martha Beck Wayfinder life coaching program. In her spare time, Karen enjoys reading, hiking, horseback riding and spending time with her husband and two children. You can learn more about Karen's work at www.karengabler.com.

Chapter 4

Epiphany on the 101

By Karen Gabler

In my twenties, I had solid plans for my life's trajectory. I would be married by age 30 and have children by age 35. I would buy a home and become a partner in a law firm by age 40. The timeline was set and I was ready to watch it unfold.

At first, my life was right on track. I married at 30, cutting it close to the wire at two months prior to my 31st birthday. I was so excited about planning my wedding day! I designed the perfect event at the ultimate location; every detail unfolded with military precision. I was the consummate princess in my ballgown wedding dress, dancing the night away and basking in the glow of being the center of attention.

I felt certain that my life was falling smoothly into place, proceeding exactly as intended. Wedding at age 30, check...next step, children! And yet, while caught up in the fervor of planning a flawless celebration, I neglected just one tiny but incredibly important detail: did I actually want to enter into the marriage that would be waiting for me after my glorious wedding?

Reality began to set in as soon as the DJ's last song ended at our reception. Our friends carried my new (drunk) husband to our hotel room, dropping him on the bed. I opened wedding cards alone in my wrinkled wedding gown while he slept. Heated confrontations began two days into our honeymoon; we fought about where to go, how to live, what to do. I looked through misty eyes at the ocean waves rolling gently onto the shore outside our hotel and wondered if I'd made a terrible mistake.

We stumbled through our first few years of marriage, trying to make the best of it. Happiness was elusive, but I took my wedding vows seriously. I had made my bed and I was prepared to lie in it. I sank into depression, spending more and more hours at work to avoid going home. When I finally gave myself permission to leave my marriage at age 34, my initial grief quickly subsided as relief washed over me. Life wasn't following the plan, but I could still get back on track.

Despite my relief, I worried about having to start over again. I had to meet someone new and build a committed relationship that would lead me back into marriage and children as soon as possible; the clock was ticking. I entered my newly single life with renewed vigor, searching for anything that would help things fall into place for me. I took a golf class, then a dance class. I went on free-spirited road trips with friends. I said "yes" to every invitation extended to me, going to parties and happy hours, meeting as many new people as possible. I met several male prospects, but none of them made me feel encouraged about my future. Several were married, telling stories about their lonely marriages to wives they never intended to divorce. One was an alcoholic; we couldn't have a conversation without several glasses of wine. A girlfriend set me up with a blind date: he spent hours over dinner telling me about his many perceived qualities until I feigned a headache and called it a night.

I began to notice a collective sense of desperation among the throngs of midlife adults searching for meaning in their cocktails and banter. My days were filled with work obligations and my nights were empty social hours. I was mentally and physically exhausted, and couldn't see a way forward to the life I thought I desired. I finally found myself sobbing in my bed, railing at the universe and demanding to know why my life felt so off-kilter. Hearing no answers, I fell into a troubled sleep.

I awoke the next morning with puffy eyes and rushed to get ready for a meeting in Los Angeles. While driving north on Highway 101 to return home, I thought about my exhaustion and despair, leading to my breakdown the night before. I thought about how much time and effort I had put into manifesting my plan for a perfect life, and how my plans were seemingly derailed at every step. I wondered why what I thought I wanted didn't seem quite as good when I received it. For the first time, I allowed myself to wonder what my life would look like if I considered an alternative plan...or, even better, had no plan at all.

Suddenly, everything around me became quiet and I felt a sense of peace wash over me. I felt the pieces of my life before me, lighting up as I considered each one. I loved my pets; they loved me unconditionally. I loved my friends; they cheered my successes and held my hand through challenges. I loved my home; it was warm and comfortable. I loved my extended family and my town and my career. I loved my classes and my weekend trips, learning new things and expanding my horizons. My life was packed with people and activities that brought me joy, and I hadn't really noticed any of it because I was so focused on searching for a committed partnership to complete my life.

I realized that my life felt full just as it was, and I was happy. I suddenly understood that I could hold both my present and my future at the same time. I could want something new to come into my life, but also feel complete right now without waiting for more. I still wanted to meet someone with whom I could have a committed relationship, but realized I didn't have to worry about when or how that might happen; it could be in a week, or a month, or a year, or five years. I still wanted children, but realized that I could have them with a partner or on my own, and it would work out at the right time and in the right way. I recognized that I didn't need a plan, and didn't have to worry about what might come into my life in the future. Instead, I could remain fully present in my current life, enjoying what I already had. I could change things I wanted to change at any time and everything could turn around in an instant. I could focus upon the here and now, letting my life unfold naturally and enjoying every minute of it as it happened.

A wide smile crossed my face and I finally felt calm. I let go of my prior distress and found myself noticing everything around me. I went to dinner with friends, loving the heartfelt conversation and laughter. I hiked with my dog, noticing the cool breeze and the soft babble of the stream alongside the trail. I went to the library and found a new book to explore. I pulled out a recipe from my cooking class and shopped for fresh, vibrant produce to include in the dish, savoring every bite of my creation. I was enjoying my life, feeling whole in the everyday moments of my days.

Three months later, Brian walked into my life. A gentle man with a warm smile that reached his loving eyes. Strong arms that enveloped me in a loving embrace. A hearty laugh as he shared jokes with me. At first, I rebelled...I just found myself! I just figured out how to be happy in my own life, and now you show up? I don't need this now! And yet, I felt a magnetic attraction to him as I looked into his eyes and felt my soul stir, saying, "Yes, of course...there you are." I made room for him in my life because I recognized the love and joy he brought to me, rather than expecting him to complete me. Twenty years later, I still feel the same magnetic attraction to him as I look into the same loving eyes while standing within the embrace of his comforting arms.

They say that you find what you want only when you finally stop looking for it. Despite the irony of finding the love of my life promptly after deciding I didn't need anything else to feel the happiness already swirling around me, I also recognize the divine beauty of finding someone to share my life only when I no longer needed someone else to make me feel whole. It can be challenging to experience joy in our lives when everything seems difficult, or when it feels like something we want is missing. And yet, even people who have been through great difficulty can find joy again by remaining present enough to notice it, allowing it to take root, and letting it exist even when something else is still missing. It is only when we stay grounded in the present, mindful of the beauty and joy around us, that we open the door to everything else awaiting us.

CHAPTER

I Always Figure It Out

Sarah Gabler

Sarah Gabler

Sarah Gabler is 19 years old and beginning her junior year of college. She is majoring in psychology with a minor in disability studies, and plans to pursue a career in counseling. Sarah is an internationally best-selling author and has been published in multiple collections of short stories. Sarah loves playing music while going on adventures with friends, as well as visiting her family in between her studies. Sarah is a lifelong artist and believes in using creativity and personal expression to facilitate strong mental health.

She began exploring self-development and soul empowerment concepts when she was just 10 years old and believes it has made her a better person today. It has motivated her to pursue her goals without fear as well as to find ways to help others on their fulfillment journey. Sarah wants to help others recognize their true potential and ensure that they feel heard, seen, and loved. She believes that everyone has a story to tell, and that bringing light to these stories can change someone's life.

Chapter 5

I Always Figure It Out

By Sarah Gabler

Life is full of lessons and transitional phases. As I am entering my junior year of college while enjoying my last year of being a teenager, I can confidently say that I have never felt more in tune with myself and the trust I hold in my path. I have watched myself grow so much over the last few years, and I see all the ways in which I have become a better person. This doesn't mean that life has been easy for me this year. In fact, during this school year, my academics have been the most challenging I've ever experienced, and my social life has been in a constant state of transition and commotion since the beginning of winter.

I've felt a great deal of pressure to be there for my friends and others while finding a way to hold onto love for myself and my own needs, all the while undergoing intense strain to keep up my GPA and the outside responsibilities and activities I hold dear. I've been incredibly busy and often overwhelmed. However, I also have never been happier with the life that I am living, and feel fully present in the most evolved version of myself so far. Above all, I have learned that I don't need to wait until I feel I have everything in place before I can decide to be happy.

Earlier in my sophomore year, after finally finding my footing and feeling proud of where I was headed, I fell into one of the most academically and emotionally challenging months of my school year. It started with a long week of intense work, studying, and chaotic energy while I crammed statistical methods and psychological disorders into my brain in preparation for my upcoming exams. This was followed by another two weeks of trying to keep up with the swirling social life around me, with multiple friends spinning through conflict in their own lives and relationships and looking to me for support.

My own mental health had taken a sharp downward spiral, and I was unsure of who or what I could trust, where I was headed, or whether I was making the right choices for myself. I was physically exhausted from my work during what felt like endless midterms. I was breaking down in every way and felt I was losing all of my progress. I was also frustrated with myself because I wanted to have my life figured out, and was deeply uncomfortable with the amount of stress rising within me on a daily basis. I knew I was better than this: why was I letting myself get bogged down in all the drama and chaos after all the work I had done on myself to change the way I walk through the world?

When I finally escaped this intense time period, I lay down on my bed in my apartment and took a deep breath. I reminded myself that my exams were done, my friends and I had resolved the ongoing conflicts among our social group, I was content with my upcoming classes in the next term of my college year, and I could feel grounded in my routine once more. As I continued to breathe, I began to play a mental slideshow of all the difficult moments I've had throughout my college experience thus far, followed by the incredible moments and memories interspersed with them.

I recalled the lessons I have learned, the meaningful friendships I have developed, and the surprises that sent me on a completely different path that ended up being better for me in the long run. I remembered the moments I thought I was at my lowest, when I was the most stressed out about an exam that ended up working out just fine, and the times I figured out how to climb back out of a hole I had dug for myself. I remembered the situations where I felt disconnected from my friends and the times I had difficult but productive conversations. I recalled the times I stood up for myself even amidst discomfort, and how much I had learned to advocate for my own well-being.

As I considered the challenging periods of my past, I recognized that I had experienced the exact same difficult feelings throughout the month that had just ended. I realized that it had felt just as hard to survive the past weeks as it had during all those past moments that seemed like mere blips in time to me now. I realized that although life has its ups and downs, and despite that some of the down periods can feel like an endless struggle, the one thing that has remained consistent in my life is that I always figure it out.

I often find myself worked up over whether or not things will work out for me, or why I am faced with ongoing difficulties. I wonder when a stressful time in my life will finally be over or how I will manage to get through it. I question whether I will ever make it out of the chaos, and wonder whether there is any point to my hurdles. While I often don't know the answer to these questions, the one thing that I know to be true as I am faced with each challenge in life is that I always manage to figure it out and keep moving forward.

We have so many moments where we are in a tailspin over something that we eventually forget about, sometimes only days later. We face challenges when we are not sure if we can pull it off, but we end up finding a solution and nailing the result. Even when we have a situation where something doesn't work out in the way we hope it will, or when we feel like everything we have ever known or wanted is falling apart, we can still find a reason that it happened as it did and discover the happiness behind that dark cloud when we drive out of the storm. No matter what circumstances arise, difficulties always pass eventually and we always figure it out.

We often forget the beauty and power found in overcoming challenges and experiencing new breakthroughs over and over again. In many moments of my life so far, I believed I had unlocked the secret to happiness after making it through a troublesome situation. Each time, I thought my new wisdom would manifest into peace and clarity going forward. And yet, I still feel surprised and overwhelmed when I am faced with a new challenge and need to figure out a way around it.

I've learned about the importance of setting boundaries, how to rely on myself when no one else could be there, how to separate my energy from that of others, how to use manifestation as a tool and not let it become a compulsion, and more. It almost feels at times like there is nothing else for me to dissect. However, there is never an end to the tools and tricks we can learn. Every person I meet can teach me something, every wall I face has a way around it that I haven't tried before, and every setback has a shortcut that leads me to better days. All of these lessons shaped me into the person I am today, and I am deeply proud of that person.

I realize now that I can attribute my growth over time to my ability to accept the feeling that I don't know what to do, as well as the possibility of figuring it out as I go. Without undergoing difficult moments, I would not have the wisdom I have today, nor would I have achieved as much as I have in my life.

In college, I have embraced the idea that I am still figuring it out, and that I will always be figuring it out. Challenges and struggles will continue to happen and will continue to shape me into a better and stronger version of myself. Accepting our ability to adapt and adjust creates deeper trust within ourselves as well as in the world around us. By remembering what we have experienced and what we have already overcome, we are able to move through these new moments with ease and compassion for ourselves and the people around us. We become better able to grasp the lessons that arise from these moments, and more equipped to use these lessons in the future.

The times I have found myself the most stressed are those moments when I forgot what I've already accomplished and doubt my ability to overcome difficult times. I've felt the most relaxed and free in my life when I have been able to let go and trust myself, even when I wasn't sure where I was going or how to get there. I know now that no matter what I must go through, I always figure it out.

CHAPTER

Six

Holding Grace in the Storm

Jaime Lee Garcia

Jaime Lee Garcia

Jaime Lee Garcia is an international bestselling author who has contributed insightful chapters in five other collaboration books through As You Wish Publishing, including *Manifestations 101 Uplifting Stories*, *The Grateful Soul*, *Wisdom Keepers*, *The Courageous Heart*, and *Own Your Awesome*. She loves to inspire others through inspirational blogs and writing, has a passion for seeing people happy, and believes making memories with your tribe is the most important thing in life. She believes perseverance is important, no matter the hardships, and most of all, to always love big. Jaime would like to thank her family and friends for their constant love and support, as they are her biggest blessings. You can reach her by email at secretwayoflife@yahoo.com or on Facebook @secretwayoflife.

Chapter 6

Holding Grace in the Storm

By Jaime Lee Garcia

"How did I get here?" I asked myself for the hundredth time, while stepping off the first plane and getting ready to jump on a final leg to my niece's wedding. I wasn't asking how I got to Burbank, as I obviously knew that. I was questioning how I reached this point in my marriage where it all crashed to the ground, while I was on an airplane heading towards my connecting flight. There are storms we must weather throughout our lives, but this one was a cyclone in my heart.

That morning, I was happily packing for my trip, excited to meet my mom, who had gone to California ahead of me. We were to begin the festivities for my niece and enjoy precious time with family and friends. Being a part of my niece's special moment was important to us, especially after the tragic and unexpected loss of my cherished brother. Knowing he would not be walking my niece down the aisle, nor enjoying his adorable baby granddaughter as she strolls down the same aisle, adorned in the cutest little flower girl dress, would be extremely hard.

The flight was emotional, as I thought about my brother and how proud he would be of his daughter. Being a Pisces and empath who soaks in emotions, I literally get sick with any sort of chaos surrounding me. So, I tend to avoid conflict, as I feel my purpose in life is to be a lover and healer. I was not prepared for the hailstorm instigated by my husband when departing the first plane. In fact, we talked that afternoon as he recounted the details of a seminar he attended. In addition, when zipping my suitcase, I had discovered a card inscribed "Wifey" on the front. It was sappy, expressing how much he loved and would miss me while I was away. I shoved the card back into my suitcase in a hurry to catch my flight.

The card had me pondering on the way to the airport. We had rocky times over the twelve years, yet a lot of fun adventures, and the birth of seven grandkids. The good times kept me believing things could turn around, that I could inspire him to be his best version, and maybe he would quit drinking if he valued our marriage enough. Reflecting on how we started and what had occurred since conflicted my emotions. The road together was not easy on my heart.

I was first married at nineteen to the father of my daughters, and we ended things amicably after twenty years. It would be four years before I reconnected with my current husband, a friend from high school. It seemed we had much in common compared to our school years. Being a non-drinker, it was important for me to find someone who wasn't one. He mentioned he rarely drank, especially since his wife passed away from alcoholism. Little did I know this was far from the truth, which would set me on a course I never imagined.

Our relationship sped forward like a silver bullet, so quickly that I was in a haze. The military brought him to Kentucky, where he retired and was determined to stay living in his secluded lake area. With support from my family, I summoned the courage to make the ultimate sacrifice of uprooting my life to start our journey together. Moving across the country was a life-altering change for me. Being close to my family, I missed them beyond words and was blessed to have my youngest daughter join me for a year. However, the change made me cry daily from missing everyone, as well as being in a secluded town where I knew no one. Keeping tears to myself, I dug deep for the courage to endure my new remote life.

Quickly, I realized that my new husband had a serious drinking problem, which he lied about. Not having the experience of dealing with it, I dreaded each time he would come home with beer. He never drank just a couple but would consume 12–16 at a time. This caused outbursts, setting my nervous system on overdrive. He would drink for any reason, such as fishing, barbecuing, yard work, and would often disappear with neighborhood friends, returning plastered drunk with erratic behaviors for me to deal with. I kept quiet, functioning on autopilot, not wanting to burden loved ones nor face the truth. I didn't move across the country to give up easily, so I held myself with class for the family by remaining silent. Recounting these issues would be throwing my husband under the bus, yet who was protecting me from emotional harm?

I felt lonely for years until my mom moved in with us from California. She was my distraction from the upheaval, but she would quickly discover the relationship I had allowed myself to remain in. It hurt her heart to see what I had settled for, and it crushed mine that she was witness to it. She relocated her life to move here, and I felt horrid at the thought of uprooting her again, especially with her cancer. So, I stayed in the marriage and continued trying to endure, at the cost of my happiness.

When would I get the courage to walk away and finally put myself first? Loved ones encouraged me to leave, especially after an event involving my very drunk husband and his handgun, terrifying three people in our home, including me. Out of respect, I hid the incident from his family, asking him to quit alcohol use and seek counseling if he wanted me to stay. My mom and I were done riding this emotional roller coaster, and I could no longer put either of us through more. Although he agreed to my terms, he continued to drink and cause chaos when I went out of town.

Time moved on until the moment I stepped off the first flight to my niece's wedding. I had minutes to eat and jump on the final leg. Excitement was building, as I could not wait to see everyone I loved and missed tremendously. Rushing through the airport, my phone repeatedly buzzed with messages. What was going on, I wondered? While glancing at my screen, my heart dropped and crashed to the floor. I had received six messages from my family, telling me that my husband had gotten drunk within hours of talking to me, had gotten in a disagreement with one, and proceeded to text each that he and I were divorcing. He did this without talking to me and only involved my family members, not his own. How do you go from getting a sappy card that morning to your marriage crumbling? After giving him continued grace and many chances to change, how can he do this to me without a single discussion? The alcohol was talking, and this time it said things it could never take back.

I knew it was over after being humiliated and hurt to the core, and I could no longer condone this behavior while looking into the eyes of those who love me. It would take courage and strength to do what was right, no matter how much it crushed me to move on.

What do you do when you find yourself in the middle of a hailstorm, and you don't know how to get out? When you're a healer, and hurting somebody goes against the core of who you are? How do you get the courage to move on and do the right thing? Well, you look at your children, your legacy, and you lead by example. You put on your big-girl pants, and you choose you, no matter what that looks like or what it takes. Dig within to find courage, to find the light, because it's always in you, ready to be ignited. Life is short and fleeting, and you must make it count. Surround yourself with those who help you thrive, so at the end of the day, you can look back and say that you lived your life with purpose and love. Always remember to shine on.

CHAPTER *Seven*

When the Dust Clears

Patricia Holgate Haney

Patricia Holgate Haney

With her husband, Gary, she continues to explore the world with insatiable curiosity and enthusiasm, reveling in the opportunities to meet new people and sharing experiences where places from pages come alive.

She enjoys time with her husband and family, which includes two sons, three grandchildren, and three great-grandchildren. She enjoys history and exploring places where history was made or where mythical stories abound.

She is a published author and an independent travel advisor, allowing her to continue her lifelong passion for sharing her memories and helping others create theirs. She helps curate travel adventures and itineraries that allow her clients to follow their dreams and passions as well.

She loves tracking seismic events and weather. She also became a weather spotter for the NWS in Arizona.

You can reach her by e-mail at
pholgatehaney@gmail.com
or seaglass@phtravels.com

Website: phtravels.com
www.amazon.com/author/patriciaholgatehaney

Chapter 7

When the Dust Clears

By Patricia Holgate Haney

There are all kinds of storms: rainstorms, thunderstorms, tornadoes, and hurricanes. Most are predictable, tracked by weather forecasters, with warnings that tell us to prepare.

Here in Arizona, we have haboobs. The first sign is always the scent, the sharp, earthy scent that tells you dust is on the wind. In the desert, storms don't just appear; they announce themselves, turning the sky dark and the air electric. The dust and leaves lift first as the wind rushes in. The dust darkens the sky in a way that is both amazing and frightening. You're suddenly surrounded by dust and debris, with no sense of direction. When the dust finally clears, it reminds us that new beginnings are possible—outside, and often within.

Life brings us storms as well. Personal storms come in many forms and at unexpected times. At times, you can see them gathering on the horizon; other times, they arrive without warning.

Can you really be prepared for a storm of a personal nature? Maybe. Sometimes it's experience, knowing you've weathered storms before and can do it again.

Sometimes it's faith. And sometimes it's just plain luck.

I don't know about you, but the small windstorms irritate me the most. If I'm not prepared, even a little dust or rain can throw me off more than the major storms—like the haboobs that roll through our desert.

Weather forecasters and emergency alerts warn you to pull over if you're driving during these storms: "Don't hit the brakes. Avoid moving forward until the storm passes." But just like with life's storms, sometimes you're already in it—and you can't avoid it.

When you're in the thick of a storm, it can feel like there's no way through. No hope. No answers. Yet most of the time, we do get through it by focusing on small, manageable steps, practicing self-compassion, and trusting that the storm will pass—even if we emerge changed.

Have you ever noticed how outside factors can affect a storm more than the storm itself? Past experiences. Your health. Relationships. Emotional exhaustion. Even hunger. All of it matters.

There's a song lyric that says, "What doesn't kill us makes us stronger." That may take things a bit too far. I don't know about you, but I'd rather not test my strength by risking not surviving at all.

We're often told that bad times give us perspective—that they keep us from becoming complacent. I understand that. Still, many of us fear losing loved ones, failing in relationships, or losing ourselves. Recognizing these fears can help us confront and manage them with compassion and resilience.

Fear of a relationship failing. Fear of another car accident. Fear of betrayal.

Fear of losing loved ones. Fear of losing myself.

I had a wise friend for over fifty years who lived to be 102. Gloria had seen extraordinary changes in her lifetime: women's rights, education, work, and relationships. Her grit and wisdom were remarkable. As she aged, she would say, "I don't know why I'm still here when others are gone, but every night I thank God, ask Him to watch over those I love, and give me the wisdom to know what I can go through."

My mother, Doris, was much the same. Her childhood wasn't the worst, but it wasn't perfect. Her parents divorced, a heavy thing in those days; her later choices led her into a difficult marriage. But she was brave and wise enough to know she didn't have to stay. Eventually, she met my father, and together they built a life and raised four children.

My mother rarely spoke of her life before him. As I got older and heard stories from relatives, I understood why. Parents of that era often shielded their children from the hard parts. We grew up believing everything was neatly tied in a bow—perfectly happy endings on television, in movies, even in our neighborhoods. The difficult times were glossed over or deleted from the stories. I sometimes think our relationships might have been healthier if we had known that real life, not fairy tales, was what we were preparing for. And real life, I believe, is better.

Growing up, I was surrounded by strong women—each shaped by different circumstances. They survived, not without scars, but with deep kindness, loyalty, and a clear understanding of how much support can matter. Some communicated openly; others remained quiet—not because they lacked strength, but because they didn't want to burden others or reveal what they believed were personal failures.

I carried that strength within myself long before I recognized it. I often used self-deprecating humor to deflect cruelty, sometimes intentional, sometimes not.

I'm not a collector of friends. I love fiercely, without expecting the same in return. Not everyone has the capacity to give what we might need in a moment, and that's okay. Not everyone is worthy of your trust and time. Often, all you need is someone to sit beside you quietly. No fixing. No words. Just presence.

I'm still learning, even at this stage of my life, to sit in silence without feeling the need to fill the space without fearing that no one will be there if I stop talking.

Surrounding yourself with people whose only motive is true friendship is one of the greatest gifts you can give yourself.

Reading, traveling, and learning—building knowledge of people, places, and ideas—strengthens the core we rely on when storms come. Stepping outside your comfort zone, sitting in your own peace, and noticing what's around you: these things feed the soul, which is the foundation of who we are.

For some, faith is the core. I have dear friends who rely fully on religion for strength. I consider myself spiritual, though I've never found one organized belief with all the answers. I look instead to the common denominators: treat others as you wish to be treated, be kind, and love builds bridges. These ideas endure because they matter—and they help us feel connected and supported.

Wisdom comes at different ages, not from a lack of effort but from experience, observation, and the roadblocks we put in our own way. Sometimes it comes from parents. Sometimes it comes from teachers, neighbors, coworkers, or strangers who briefly cross our path and leave a mark.

When you think you have it bad, whether it is health, relationships, or circumstances, there is almost always someone struggling more. That may sound simplistic, but gratitude matters not just for the good times, but for what you've weathered.

Share your experience, but don't tell others what should work for them. Listen. Be a sounding board. Offer hugs when needed. Laugh "with" never "at." Find humor where you can.

Be like my friend Gloria. Be like my mother, Doris. Be like the school nurse who noticed.

Be like the aunt who remembered what you survived. Be like my husband, who shows love through action, lifts me, and allows me to be myself—something that takes its own kind of courage.

When the storm passes, you dry the tears, clean up what you can, and remember: you made it through. You're a little better prepared for the next one—because there will always be another storm. Not necessarily stronger, just different.

I believe angels walk among us. I've met several. They've reminded me of a higher power and of human kindness acting on its behalf. Watch for the signs. Feel the warmth. Answer the quiet tug on your heart. Be an earthly angel for someone else. We don't have to wait for immortality to do good.

Most of all, be kind to yourself. Believe in yourself. Give yourself grace. You're not meant to be perfect—just present, honest, and trying.

Storms will come. There's no forecast for them. But know this: you will survive. And when the dust clears, you may find yourself seeing the world—and yourself—with new eyes.

I have so far—and every time the dust clears, I discover a little more strength, a little more clarity, and a deeper appreciation for the calm that follows. After the storm, I know now: I'm changed, I'm here, and I'm ready for whatever comes next.

CHAPTER

From Crisis to Triumph

Foxye Brown Jackson

Foxye Brown Jackson, BSN, RN

Foxye Brown Jackson, BSN, RN, is a four-time best-selling author, international speaker, Reiki Master, life coach, nurse leader, and passionate community advocate dedicated to helping others heal and thrive. As the anchoring host of P.E.A.C.E. with Foxye, she shares compassionate, practical guidance for survivors of sexual assault and domestic and interpersonal violence, creating spaces where pain can transform into power.

Her published works include contributions to *Inspirations: 101 Uplifting Stories for Daily Happiness*, *Manifestations: True Stories of Bringing the Imagined Into Reality*, and *Enduring Wisdom: Life Insights That Stand the Test of Time*, as well as her deeply personal solo memoir, *Lies and Lullabies: Healing My Fragmented Soul*, which includes actionable steps to facilitate healing from abuse, abandonment, and grief.

Holding bachelor's degrees in psychology and nursing and currently pursuing a Master of Science in Nursing, Foxye blends clinical expertise with lived experience to guide others toward holistic healing—mind, body, and spirit. Her mission is to be a beacon of light, reminding people of their resilience and our shared interconnectedness.

Through storytelling, service, and creative empowerment, she inspires others to reclaim their voices, rediscover their strength, and live well—fully, courageously, and on purpose.

YouTube: www.youtube.com/@peacewithfoxye
Reach Foxye via email: peacewithfoxye@gmail.com

Chapter 8

From Crisis to Triumph

By Foxye Brown Jackson

"You're in a crisis..."

Whenever I think about my healing progress, it always begins with this phrase spoken by my therapist during our first session. Thinking back to that moment, I can still feel the weight of life encircling my chest, squeezing me like a life vest—meant to keep me alive, yet preventing me from taking a full breath. The shallow breathing and excessive crying resulted in dizziness that compounded the vise grip around my head. I ran to the bathroom for a towel in response to the tears that soaked my face and ran down my neck to my clothing. My nose became red and dripped with the overflow of emotion. I wanted to hide from the camera, but being visible to my therapist was a requirement of virtual therapy. I want to say I felt hopeless in that moment, but it was much more than that. I felt desperate for a swift and permanent escape from reality because I had no idea how to move from crisis to triumph.

In preparing for this chapter, I reread my old journals and realized I had been battling suicidal ideation since childhood. It started when my great-uncle became aware of my sexual abuse and moved me to live with his family. Their religion proposed that prayer and fasting were the answer to everything. In fact, they were supposed to alleviate the impulsive and intrusive thoughts of suicide. They did not, and, eventually, I was court-ordered to attend therapy. I was resistant to therapy and vowed not to participate because it was not my choice. Unfortunately, that need for escape remained consistent into adulthood, and I did not realize how much help I needed until I had the courage to ask for it.

By the time I reached this adult moment in my therapy session, I had endured decades of sexual, physical, and emotional violence. There were also periods of poverty, food scarcity, and residential moves across county and state lines to ensure the safety of my children, who were born during my marriages. Even that clarification reveals religious oppression; I felt compelled to say I was married to avoid the judgment placed on women who become pregnant while unwed.

Speaking up for myself often led to maltreatment from elders, women, family members, and others I believed would be supportive of my stance against abuse. Instead, they supported things like barring me from participating in the local Debutante for teenage girls, because they believed I was not pure anymore after my stepfather had sex with me. These layers of abuse, judgments, and oppression carved out a deep pit of isolation and loneliness within me.

Humans are communal beings, and being socially ostracized made me feel the only safe place was within myself, and even that space was tarnished with suicidal thoughts. Sexual and physical abuse are tangible. Psychological abuse is more like abstract art used to cover an unwanted tattoo; one can tell something is off, but can't pinpoint the truth. A skilled artist can manipulate the tattoo—the situation—so that even the person wearing it can't tell where the covered art exists. That was my mind state and I needed someone to decipher truth for me.

I did not start therapy because of suicidal ideations, nor the feelings of isolation I had endured over the years. I started therapy because I needed to know whether I was crazy. I understand the word crazy is outdated and inappropriate. In my state of crisis, my mind reached for words that seemed most accurate to describe me to me. I had a degree in psychology and provided professional care to people with mental health diagnoses. Yet, I felt confused, embarrassed, and disheartened by my current mental state. Even now, tears threaten to blind my vision as I think back to what it felt like to be a victim of such abuse.

The man I was married to when I started therapy often rearranged facts, twisted my words, and minimized my claims of emotional abuse. He would become angry with me and stop acknowledging my presence whenever I shared my perspective or disagreed with him, and then deny that he was giving me the silent treatment. After days away from home, he would blame me for our lack of time together. He never chose to take accountability for his actions. Instead, he used sarcasm and jokes to ridicule me, followed by insincere apologies meant to invalidate my hurt. The inconsistent wavelength of love and support he claimed to provide caused my inner thoughts to fluctuate between believing he loved me, believing I needed to leave him, and believing I may be overthinking everything. In the middle of it all were my children and my need to prevent them from normalizing abuse in their relationships.

Since my early twenties, my children have been the reason I chose not to end my life—and they still are—but I wanted to live for myself, too. I wanted to reach a place where I loved and valued my own existence as much as others valued me. I wanted to be my own light on the days when disappointment and fear darkened the sky and that crushing weight returned to my chest. That is what I set out to do.

My therapist became my guide on my healing journey. I made the decision to separate from my husband, followed by the finality of divorce. The choice to go through with the divorce was difficult because I had married him believing we would spend our lives together. As months passed, love eroded and his hypocrisies grew more obvious. He continued the silent treatment, left me struggling to pay household bills while hiding money behind false claims of scarcity, and criticized anyone who grew close enough to empower me. Near the end, he became a consistent catalyst for suicidal ideations.

Every fear I had run from as I grew into womanhood, and every silent battle I had fought, culminated in this perfect storm my therapist called a crisis. I continued therapy after the divorce and uncovered other areas that needed a healing touch. At one point, overwhelmed, I asked my therapist, "Why do I pay you to do this to me?" It seemed that every time I thought I was improving, something would send me spiraling back into the dark abyss of desiring an escape from the immense emotional pangs. However, I knew there was no room in my current journey for the angst, fear, or self-deprecation I had carried throughout life like unrelenting baggage. It was time to unpack.

Through cognitive behavioral therapy, Eye Movement Desensitization and Reprocessing (EMDR), and spiritual practices, my therapist and I uncovered negative beliefs and patterns associated with my complex post-traumatic stress disorder (cPTSD), depression, and anxiety. I gave myself permission to unpack, to be different, and I began to flirt with being triumphant. Each week, I unpacked more emotional baggage and relished the newfound freedom to love myself wholly.

That husband—one of three—turned my world upside down. Escaping his grip gave me space to breathe again and gave my children the safety they needed to share with me the horrors they experienced because of him. Their truths devastated me and filled me with guilt for ever marrying him. I believed he would keep us safe and that he would teach and guide us. I trusted him when he said he cared. In the end, he was only capable of producing external turmoil that mirrored his internal war of trauma and anger. It is often said that hurting people hurt others, and I had to choose whether I would be the hurting person who hurts others. By others, I mean me.

It is difficult to fight in a battle when you have not been trained to be a warrior. The fear, uncertainty, and lack of confidence that stem from abuse cloud the psyche and create a veil that convinces you that you are incapable. Deep down, I still believed I was capable of anything despite my experiences, for I was uniquely designed to bring light to the world and peace to communities. I trained with my therapist and became self-aware of my early signs of depression. I delved into learning about myself as if I were a new partner. I scheduled time with myself and embraced triumph over crisis with the understanding that living is a daily source of gratitude. Though we may endure both crisis and triumph, we have a choice whether to do it alone or with help. The triumph is in becoming a warrior of life who chooses to accept help.

CHAPTER

The Storm That Set Me Free

Dr. Donna Kiel

Dr. Donna Kiel

Dr. Donna Kiel is a life coach, consultant, professor, and former school leader whose work helps people rediscover the courage, clarity, and purpose that often get buried beneath the pressures of everyday life. Those who work with Donna frequently describe the experience as transformational—not because she tells them what to do, but because she has a remarkable ability to help people see themselves more clearly and step into the lives they truly want to lead.

With a background in psychology, counseling, and leadership, Donna brings a rare combination of professional expertise and deeply human insight to her coaching. Her approach blends compassion, wisdom, humor, and what many affectionately call her "Kieled" style—a way of gently but powerfully helping people shift their thinking, release old fears, and discover new possibilities for their lives.

Clients often come to Donna feeling stuck, overwhelmed, or unsure of their next step. Through thoughtful conversation, deep listening, and practical guidance, she helps them reconnect with their strengths, trust their voice, and move forward with confidence. The result is not simply problem-solving, but genuine life transformation—greater peace, stronger relationships, renewed purpose, and the courage to live authentically.

Donna holds a BA in Psychology, an MA in Counseling, and a Doctorate in Leadership. Over the course of her career, she has supported thousands of individuals, educators, and leaders around the world in creating lives of meaning and impact.

She can be reached at drdonnakiel@gmail.com or www.donnakiel.com

Chapter 9

The Storm That Set Me Free

By Dr. Donna Kiel

Most of my life, I've wanted to feel safe, connected, and, honestly, liked—very liked. I've never liked the term 'people pleaser.' It sounds weak and desperate, which never captured my experience. A more accurate description: I was a professional emotional weather forecaster, able to read a room faster than the Weather Channel reads a radar map.

Before anyone said a word, I could feel the shift in the air. A tightening in someone's jaw meant irritation was brewing. A pause in conversation meant disappointment had entered the room. A slightly raised eyebrow meant someone was about to disagree but was still deciding whether it was worth the effort. If emotional weather had a Doppler system, I would have been the meteorologist standing in front of it, pointing to a swirling mass and saying, "Yes, we can see a storm forming here—but don't worry, I'll handle it."

I could sense when someone needed reassurance, encouragement, or simply to feel important. I could also sense when tension was building and quietly step in to smooth things out before the storm arrived. If someone seemed overwhelmed, I offered to help. If someone looked frustrated, I softened the edges of the situation. If someone had too much on their plate, I often volunteered to take something off it—sometimes before they even finished asking.

Empathy came naturally to me, but it evolved into something more complicated along the way. Instead of simply understanding how others felt, I began stepping fully inside their emotions. I set my own feelings aside and absorbed theirs. If someone was anxious, I felt responsible for helping them calm down. If someone was upset, I believed it was my job to restore peace. If someone felt disappointed, I quietly took it upon myself to fix whatever had gone wrong.

In other words, my empathy slowly turned into emotional shape-shifting. I adjusted who I was depending on what the moment required. If someone needed reassurance, I became reassuring. If someone needed calm, I became calm. If someone needed someone to take responsibility for a difficult situation, I stepped forward.

And I did not just say yes when people asked for help. Often, I volunteered before anyone even asked. Someone needed a committee chair. I could do that. Someone needed an event organized. I would handle it. Someone needed a difficult conversation managed. I could take care of that, too.

It was not that people forced these responsibilities on me. In many cases, I offered. Being helpful felt like being valuable, and being valuable felt like being safe. Looking back, I realize my empathy had quietly crossed a line. Instead of simply understanding others, I had begun organizing my life around making sure they never felt uncomfortable.

Ironically, this skill set served me very well professionally. I became a school counselor, then director of counseling, and eventually an assistant principal. My ability to understand people, resolve conflicts, and anticipate problems before they escalated made me effective in leadership roles. Parents trusted me. Teachers confided in me. Students came to my office because they knew I would listen.

I built an entire career on understanding what people needed and responding quickly.

Looking back, I did not realize I was losing my sense of self while trying to please others. The need for approval was quietly erasing my voice.

For seventeen years, I said yes. Yes to administrators. Yes to teachers. Yes to parents. Yes to students. I said yes to late-night meetings, unexpected crises, new initiatives, extra committees, and responsibilities that quietly accumulated until my days stretched far beyond anything resembling balance. My schedule is filled with everyone else's priorities, and somehow that feels normal.

In fact, it felt successful. People appreciated me. They trusted me. They relied on me. I was the calm in everyone else's storm.

What I did not understand yet was that underneath that calm lived a quiet fear of disappointing people. If someone was upset with me, something inside me felt wrong. That fear kept me constantly adjusting, constantly accommodating, constantly making sure everyone around me felt supported.

I lived this way for seventeen years until one moment cracked the whole system open.

The principal was out of town, which meant that as assistant principal, I was in charge. If you have ever worked in a school, you know that being "in charge" usually means something interesting is about to happen. A teacher came to my office, visibly shaken. A student had made a comment in class that "anyone could bring a gun to school." The Columbine tragedy had happened not long before, and schools everywhere were on edge. The teacher was frightened and demanded that the student be expelled immediately.

I gathered the information and met with the student. She was distraught. She admitted saying it but insisted she had not meant it as a threat. As we talked, she began sobbing and explained what was happening in her life. Her parents were divorcing, her home life was unstable, and school was the one place she felt connected. She had said something reckless because she wanted attention.

Before making a final decision, I called the principal. I explained the situation and recommended that we require a psychological assessment and counseling, and allow her to remain in school. The principal agreed. I contacted the student's mother, explained the plan, arranged the counseling support, and believed we had handled the situation responsibly.

A week later, the principal returned. After speaking with the teacher, she called me into her office and told me the student needed to be expelled. Parents had called expressing fear, and the pressure had changed the decision.

In that moment, I felt the familiar surge of anxiety I had experienced many times before. My instincts knew exactly what to do: smooth it over, agree, restore calm.

But something inside me stopped.

For the first time in my life, I said no.

I explained that I had assured the student and her family that she would not be expelled. I had told them we cared about her and wanted her to receive help. Reversing that decision now felt wrong.

The principal expelled the student anyway, and she was furious with me.

Every instinct in my body wanted to repair the relationship. I knew exactly how to do it. I could simply agree with her decision. I could say I had misjudged the situation. I could smooth the entire conflict over with one sentence.

But I could not do it.

Instead, I did something I had never done before. I sat with the fear—fear of losing my job, fear of disappointing someone whose approval I had sought for years, fear of rejection.

Underneath that fear was something deeper; it was shame. The quiet belief that if someone was angry with me, I must have done something terribly wrong.

So, I allowed the fear to stay. I did not run from it. I simply let it exist.

A few days later, the principal asked me. Before the meeting, I wrote a resignation letter, sealed it in an envelope, and walked into her office.

She began the meeting by saying, "This is very difficult to say."

I raised my hand gently and stopped her.

"I resign," I said, sliding the envelope across the desk.

In that moment, something happened. I was free. Not because the situation was easy and not because I knew what would come next, but because, for the first time, I chose my truth over approval.

That moment did not transform me into a fearless person. I had years of learning ahead. But it opened a door I did not know existed.

The real shift came years later when I became a grandmother. Holding that little girl changed how I saw everything. I began asking myself what kind of example I wanted to set for her. Did I want her to grow up believing her job was to keep everyone comfortable? Did I want her to organize her life around other people's approval? No. I wanted her to grow into a woman who trusted her voice, valued her feelings, and knew her worth did not depend on keeping everyone happy. If I wanted that for her, I had to learn to live it myself.

I stopped running from fear and learned to sit with it. Most of us spend enormous energy trying to avoid the things we fear most—disapproval, rejection, failure. But fear is rarely the storm we imagine it to be.

When we stop running and allow the feeling to exist, it begins to lose its power. And in the quiet that follows, something remarkable appears—our own voice.

For most of my life, I believed my job was to forecast everyone else's emotional weather and keep the skies clear. Now I understand something better. Storms come. Storms pass. But sometimes the very storm we fear is the storm that sets us free.

CHAPTER

Walking With Divinity

Becki Koon

Becki Koon

Becki Koon is an International Bestselling Author and Speaker, Heart-based Energy Intuitive, Holy Fire III® Karuna Reiki Master, HeartMath® Coach, Life Coach, ThetaHealer®, Crystal Practitioner, and ULC Minister. Becki empowers people to seek inner wisdom, holding space for them to discover and grow into the next highest version of themselves. She does this through a compassionate, loving presence. Becki views her service as a sacred gift from God.

In sessions, Becki receives support and guidance from Jesus, angelic guides, family of light, other people's guides, loved ones who've passed, Gaia, ascended masters, and God. Channeling is a gift, she says, that helped save her life from the depths of grief and personal challenge. She thanks God for every breath she takes and is honored to offer that divine energy to her clients.

Contact:

stepstone2you@gmail.com
www.beckikoon.com

Chapter 10

Walking with Divinity

By Becki Koon

The room I am standing in echoes with the memory of a life gone, no longer part of the reality I find myself living. Strange how I feel: relief for the lifting of a vision created by two and carried out by one; easing the burden of a promise made only by me to carry on the dream envisioned well before Jack died. I breathe in the scent of dust stirred up by moving, packing into boxes treasures of experiences that now carry tears of letting go, of moving on. I wander through rooms devoid of the creation two deeply-in-love people manifested. I stand in a space no longer full of opportunity but a reminder that life can turn on a dime. I ask myself how I will survive another huge change, another letting go of deeply held convictions, and creation.

I take a deep breath. Can I really take all my precious rocks, stones, and crystals to storage? My quick answer, *yes!* Call me the crazy rock lady, but some part of me cries for constancy, taking the solid form of memories with me, even if it is to a small storage unit until I settle.

Interesting, the concept of being settled. Looking back over the last ten years, shoot, if I'm honest, over most of my life, it wouldn't appear settled or stable to someone looking at outward appearances. Boring is a word I could never claim. Intense, yes. I claim intense. Full of hardship, yes, but my definition of hardship is mine, which may not be in resonance with someone else's idea. Full of heartache, a resounding *yes*, but I also embrace my heart's full expression without judgment, for to feel fully, no matter the high or low, is to be unapologetically alive.

Wisdom pours through the acceptance that life is ever changing, ever evolving, and ever growing, whether we understand it at the time or not. It is a gift we all get to embrace if we choose. But how? How is it that I can stand in a room that echoes with the memory of a life gone by and find relief, while at the same time shedding tears of loss? How do we as humans allow the storms of life to blow on through without the torrent of energy destroying us?

I do not want to come across as simplifying a very complex concept, as we each have a unique experience of our life force, an individuated spark of the divine, God, universal life force. But what I can do is share my life wisdom, my genuine heart, my written words with you as we journey together on this beautiful planet lovingly referred to as Gaia.

When I sit back, quiet my mind, and allow my heart to lead me, I find the act of acceptance is inextricably linked to awareness of purpose. Something inside of me has always whispered, I was meant to be here, on the planet, at this time of evolution. I have never doubted my presence or the truth of that understanding. Perhaps being born premature and fighting for my life from the very beginning moments of breath gave me a determined essence by which the very fact of survival cemented that truth deep in my bones, into my being.

Love has always come easily to me. Don't judge me for saying those words. I never remember a time I didn't love life. Again, my love of life and my experience of life are often two completely diverging movements on opposite ends of the spectrum. What is it in me that can live a challenged life, experience ferocious storms, yet love it so wholeheartedly?

I never lost my connection to God. Is it really that simple? Yes and no, a full encompassing of the spectrum of life! But one fact is without reproach: I survived. And I continued to survive every trauma, every heartbreak, every downturn, every challenge, walking with the greatest love I have ever experienced outside of my family, God. I never lost God.

When I was 15, I had an experience with Jesus, or Yeshua in the original Hebrew/Aramaic, that was so deeply personal and physically real, I can recall it as if it were happening to me now. I've heard people describe the experience of receiving the Holy Spirit or connecting to the higher divine self. It falls into the realm of the indescribable, but let me be vulnerable and paint a picture of what my body feels when in communion with divinity. Many people have asked me how I know I am connected, and what it feels like, curious to know if they can feel it too.

I have a deep yearning within my soul to share this energetic experience with you and take you on the journey with me. I have learned not to question myself when I feel these strong urges. And truly, this is how I survive all that comes my way. It is my greatest hope that you find an even deeper connection to your divine self, a sacred communion to guide you through the more difficult aspects of life.

There is a delicious moment that occurs when I make a connection to God, Jesus, and the sacred divine within me. When there, my essence is in a place of interwoven relationship to a wisdom beyond my human mind. It is as if the knowledge of that moment is key to all reality, the answer to my very existence. The design of my human life is perfect, and in divine communion, no matter the circumstances, I feel completely at peace. The stormy winds can be howling around me, and the calm in the eye of the storm is my countenance.

Often, my eyes are closed, and my awareness drops into my breath, into my heart. I feel the rise and fall of my chest and allow the subtle field of energy around me to knock on the door of my body. The skin on my arms begins to sense ever-so-subtle temperature changes, and often I feel movement, as if a slight breeze has just arisen. My mind clears, and I talk to God, in a state of gratitude for each breath, for the life force pulsing through my body. Then I feel him, Jesus comes close to me, I see a beautiful vision of him in his sacred radiance, his eyes gazing at me with a love beyond human definition. My heart feels like it's been blasted open to receive this kind of outpouring of love, and tears well up automatically. I can't help but cry tears of complete surrender to the wave of compassionate light and love beginning to wash over me. My body begins to vibrate, as if each cell is oscillating at a high frequency to meet him. My mind calms, my body adjusts, and my intuitive sight opens, the top of my head tingling with sacred energy as it infuses my physical form. The bliss that encompasses me is all-consuming, and any sense of separation from Jesus melts away. I am one with him, my heart and his beat in tandem. I know him with every fiber of my being. I do not question, feeling the perfection of it all as the waves of divinity wash over me, through me. Often, it takes my breath away for a moment, as the feeling is powerful and my chest feels the pressure. Then, with the next deep breath taken, the wave moves through my body once more, raising my light, my body tingling with a high-frequency joy. I am home in this moment, in full remembrance of who I am and why.

The desire to be in that divine love grows stronger each day, and the ability to share this compassion with others is my way of walking with God and honoring the divine gift of life bestowed upon me. The passage I just described and walked you through can happen over hours, minutes, or in an instant. There is no right or wrong way to work with the sacred divine within. Every day lived experiences become like a walking prayer while magic abounds. Even the darkest hardships become opportunities to dive into being fully human, living the medicine wheel of co-creation.

Can you see how this has assisted me whenever the struggles of life surround me? Probably the most profound moment of clarity came with the death of my beloved husband, Jack. We had 20 days to perform the hardest act any of us face when losing a loved one, saying goodbye, knowing full well life will never be the same again. The one thing we did together was work with the sacred divinity we knew we could access. As the days flew by and his body started to give way, we honored him, his passage into life after life. We performed gargantuan tasks by walking hand in hand with his failing body and the divine source energy surrounding us. From somewhere deep in my body, I knew we were being held in sacredness, compassionate love, and light. Jesus was my rock as I cried out in excruciating grief, holding Jack when he took his last breath.

We were blessed to traverse the death passage while at home. Hospice and my mom were ever-present when needed. Friends offered love, food, companionship, and a shoulder. When Jack transitioned, I called the mortuary after we had spent about three hours with him. I was gifted the opportunity to say goodbye, rubbing sacred oils on his still body, changing his clothes, sharing stories with my mom and a dear friend, and slowly getting ready for the inevitable taking away of his physical form. The two morticians came and were taken aback by the feel in the room. They could not help but notice the presence of divine sacredness and love radiating throughout. They were drawn in by my demeanor and mentioned they were honored to witness death in such a sacred container with such grace. In fact, one of the gentlemen contacted me later with a unique request. He asked if he could bring his wife by my place so she could see for herself the room in which Jack was honored while going home. When the mortician got home late that night after taking Jack to the mortuary, his wife did not believe he had just taken in a body; the smell on him was of beautiful, sacred oils. She had never had that happen and was surprised, so he couldn't help but show her the place of sacred passage.

Twenty months later, I was diagnosed with aggressive stage-3 breast cancer. Once again, I felt the opportunity to reach even deeper into my connection to Jesus, God, the divine. I was never upset with my body or the cancer. I remember feeling the hot flush of shock when I heard the doctor utter the word cancer. It was the familiar flush, as when Jack and I heard the same word in the emergency room with his doctor, except she tenderly added the word 'terminal'.

I knew I had to face myself. I could have easily decided to move on from this life, allowing my body to take me down the passage of no return. Cancer was present to show me how committed I was to life. It showed me how to love deeper than I had ever known. In fact, I talked to my body, the cancer cells, and this is what they shared with me in channel writing.

"We are not to be feared, to be at war with. Love us into non-existence. Love us into a transformational energy that cleanses the heart and soul and changes lives. Complete love of self is key. Can you love that completely, that fully, your body that shows you the pocket of unwellness in your soul? We only exist as a modifier of energy, a catalyst for the body, mind, and soul, to shift, to change, to expand, into something new. It is your choice."

Choice, it was my choice? I was shocked, and yet some part of me knew a higher level of wisdom. We all get to experience personal crossroads, defining moments when we feel like we walk alone, no one else able to make the decision for us or take the action only we can take. But here's the truth. *We are never alone!*

I am reminded of the famous poem, "Footprints In The Sand" by Mary Stevenson in 1939. There are numerous versions of that poem, but one visual stands out, a single set of footprints shown walking along the beach, where there were once two. The premise is that a man has a dream, he is walking with the Lord through his life, and there are always two sets of footprints in the sand. He has no doubt; he knows the Lord is with him. Then, during the most difficult times in his life, he looks back and finds a single set of footprints in the sand. Thinking the Lord abandoned him during the most difficult times in life, he asks why? Lord, why did you abandon me when I needed you most? The Lord replied to him, "It was during the most difficult times of your life that I carried you. You were never alone but loved and supported beyond measure."

I have been carried by Jesus and God, the angels, my guides, and my higher soul-self so many times I don't care to count. But that is the point. Part of the beauty of this planet is the actively dynamic life force of growth, movement, and evolution, which creates storms of renewal, freshness, and change. We often navigate those storms with a compass designed with one purpose: to show us the way. What if the very compass you are seeking is already with you? What if the compass you seek is waiting for you to reach out and connect with it? And, what if that compass has nothing but love for you and is carrying you across the most difficult shores of life?

The energy exchange is real. The love wave is tangible; it shifts awareness, changes the thought process, and guides with a wisdom not of the thinking, repetitive mind but of the higher mind, the one connected to divinity. It is from the divine mind that peace pervades chaos, and the strength to weather whatever storms present becomes a power stance.

Imagine a world in which we all knew our connection to God and the divine within, knowing that all aspects of our human experience were part of the play, gathering wisdom, and picking up a few rocks along the way. Survival then becomes a dance, and the aspect of living, no matter the intensity of the storm, becomes a joy! In the end, what survives the storm is you, divine and beautifully human you!

CHAPTER

Eleven

The Gift of Loss

Bradley Kovacevich

Bradley Kovacevich

Bradley Kovacevich lives in Northern California, grounded by the strength of her community. Following the profound loss of her son just before his eleventh birthday, she found herself drawn to the mystical. She embarked on a healing and transformative journey of spiritual discovery. A graduate of the Academy of Intuition Medicine®, Bradley is a seeker of the sacred and the unseen, curious about all that lies beyond ordinary perception. Her study of mediumship is a natural extension of a life shaped by healing, wonder, and the threshold between worlds.

Chapter 11

The Gift of Loss

By Bradley Kovacevich

May 23, 2013, is the day my life split in two: a before and an after I never saw coming.

The night before, our nine-year-old son Joey vomited after dinner. Thinking it was a stomach bug, I kept him home. While I took his sister to school, he slept in my bed. With our contractor at the house for a construction project, I didn't worry about leaving Joey. Later, when I tried to wake him, he answered in jumbled, nonsensical words. At first, I thought he was joking, but after a few more questions, I realized something was very wrong. I called my husband, who rushed home, and together we took Joey to the emergency room. Something in me knew, even then, we were driving toward a moment we would never fully come back from. Our lives would never be the same.

Joey, his sister, and I had planned a Memorial Day weekend trip to Palm Springs with two other moms and their children. That plan dissolved into something unimaginable. At the hospital, Joey was diagnosed with a brain tumor and needed emergency surgery. Weeks later, we learned the heartbreaking truth: Joey had glioblastoma, a deadly brain cancer. Doctors told us he likely had less than two years to live. Nothing prepares you for those words. In that moment, I felt like I was suffocating. I understood I would outlive my son. The room felt still. Everything looked the same, but nothing ever would be again. The grief begins before the loss.

He battled valiantly for fourteen months.

After Joey's passing, I knew my husband, our daughter, and I would need counseling. The very idea of it filled me with dread. I believed talk therapy kept a person stuck in the past, rehashing events. I went because it was expected. Attending therapy signaled to others that I was doing the right things, moving in the right direction, and being the best mother and wife I could be.

In my first session, I told the therapist about some of the signs I'd received from Joey since his passing. Small, undeniable moments of connection that told me he was still here, still present in some form. She listened, then said, with clinical matter-of-factness, "You realize he is dead, don't you?" Her response told me everything I needed to know. I did not go back. To this day, signs from Joey continue to comfort me and let me know he is still around.

A friend eventually connected me with a new therapist. I tried a few sessions. In what turned out to be our final meeting, he said, “One day you will see the gift in Joey’s passing.” I was horrified. How could there possibly be a gift in losing my beloved boy? Devastated, I left and did not return to him or any other therapist.

Years later, I began to understand what he meant. I could see a multitude of gifts Joey’s passing had revealed. These gifts had always existed, but I had moved through life too quickly and too comfortably to fully see. Surprisingly, I felt something I hadn’t expected: gratitude. Gratitude for this therapist, and for the words that had once enraged me.

Joey gave every person he met the gift of seeing the beauty in themselves. Even at his sickest, when someone asked how he was doing, he would smile and say “awesome,” then immediately turn the spotlight onto them, finding something specific and wonderful to point out. Only after he was gone did I realize how rare it truly was. He was always wise beyond his years, innately understanding people and making everyone feel as though they had known him forever. Both children and adults gravitated toward him. He was a connector, bringing unlikely friends together and making sure nobody was ever left out. Parents of children he had just met would seek me out afterward, pressing notes with their contact information into my hand, hoping to arrange a playdate. Something about Joey made every first meeting feel like the beginning of a lifelong friendship.

Joey taught everyone what it means to be resilient. He faced one of the most devastating diagnoses a person can receive with grace and bravery, never complaining as the cancer stripped away every part of him. As his body deteriorated, Joey remained himself, never once conveying sadness or frustration over what he was losing. He faced the unimaginable with a grace that left everyone around him quietly changed. When you witness your child meet the unthinkable that way, something shifts inside you permanently. It becomes the standard by which you measure your own strength for the rest of your life.

After Joey passed, my husband, our daughter, and I faced a choice. We could remain in misery and heartbreak, or we could live like Joey. We knew that staying paralyzed by grief would dishonor everything he had taught us. Joey lived every minute to the fullest, and to stop living would be to betray him. We discovered something we never could have learned any other way. Loss, as devastating as it is, cuts through everything that once felt important and reveals only what matters most.

We became involved with an organization in our community that serves as a home away from home for out-of-town families whose children are receiving treatment for cancer and life-threatening illnesses. We immersed ourselves in the organization, spending time with families doing crafts, playing games, preparing and serving meals, and celebrating Joey's birthday each year with a special dinner. My husband joined the board, and I co-chair an annual fundraising event that raises critical funds to support its mission. Among these families, we sometimes encounter children with diagnoses similar to Joey's. We never share that Joey had not survived unless we are asked. We know what it feels like to need hope more than anything else. When your child is fighting for their life, hope is all you have. Every family deserves the chance to believe their child will be the exception, and it is not our place to take that from them. Instead, we hold space and let them feel less alone. Being present for them without sharing our own story is its own form of love. What began as a way to honor Joey became a gift that continues to heal and sustain us.

We also created a social innovation fellowship in Joey's name within the school community he adored. Joey's mind was always in motion. He was a natural design thinker and inventor, drawn not just to the spark of a new idea, but to the deeper question of what that idea could do to improve the world. Each year, Joey's father, sister, and I join a committee of faculty who knew him to select students who have designed something to solve a real-world problem. The fund takes their projects from prototype into action, and meeting the fellowship applicants each year has become one of the most healing parts of our grief journey. Connecting with young people who share Joey's passion for solving the world's problems, we catch glimpses of him everywhere. Their belief that one person can make a difference is so deeply familiar.

In these moments, Joey feels very close. In many of those students, we find a piece of Joey we were afraid we might lose, and we feel most certain that his work in this world is not finished.

Joey's short life created a legacy that continues to unfold in ways we did not plan and could not have predicted. Joey came into this world with something to teach, and he taught it completely in ten and three-quarter years. His essence is etched into the lives of everyone he touched.

As I watch Joey's peers reach milestones he never had the chance to achieve, I find consolation in the question his life implicitly answered every single day: What will my gifts to the world be? Loss has a way of making that question more urgent in a way that comfort never can. Of all the gifts Joey's passing revealed, that question may be the most enduring and unexpected of all. Joey answered it every single day he was alive, so effortlessly and so completely that he never needed to speak it aloud. He always knew.

CHAPTER

Twelve

He Chose Me, and I Chose Him

Jennifer Lahey

Jennifer Lahey

Jennifer Lahey is a New York City-based coach, parent educator, and meditation leader whose work centers on helping clients create calmer, more connected relationships in all areas of their lives and discover and live their purpose. Trained in multiple modalities—including the Enneagram, mindfulness and meditation, and reflective, values-based coaching—she works with individuals and families coast to coast in a deeply personalized, growth-oriented process.

After earning her MBA and beginning her career in the media business, she chose to step fully into family life, raising her three children while contributing extensively as a community volunteer and nonprofit board member.

Now in a meaningful second chapter, Jennifer supports parents of both neurotypical and neurodiverse children as they move from reactivity to reflection and from struggle to greater ease and understanding, while also coaching adults seeking greater clarity, alignment, and transformation in their own lives. She is the co-founder of Terra Meditations, where she leads live guided meditation experiences. Jennifer lives in New York City with her husband.

Chapter 12

He Chose Me, and I Chose Him

By Jennifer Lahey

The moment of panic and realization came as I drove away from home one evening, alone in my car, driving just to get away. The signs had become too clear to ignore that our eighteen-month-old son had serious developmental delays. Something wasn't right. Outside, it was pitch black, with just the occasional streetlight and no other cars on the road. What makes this memory so vivid twenty-plus years later is that I was both driving my car and watching the entire scene from above. I was split in half, both inside my body and outside of it at the same time. I was the main character at the wheel and the observer flying overhead—both embodying and witnessing the frightened mother moving forward alone through the darkness.

This experience in the car became an apt metaphor for my early journey as the mother of a neurodiverse child. There were so many questions with no ready answers. In an environment filled with uncertainty and obscurity, could I chart a steady path forward for my son, as his mother and advocate? And just as importantly, could I elevate my perspective to function as a wise and compassionate observer—of him, of myself, and of our circumstances? Although fear was my primary fuel in those early days, could I trade in the anxiety for faith that things would actually be okay, whatever that might mean?

Life with Paul, our first child, was an enjoyable adventure during his first year of life. We moved from New York to London when he was six months old and were immersing ourselves in this vibrant capital city. Paul and I spent our days strolling around South Kensington, taking swim classes, and visiting the science museum's play area. We took advantage of our location to travel with Paul to Paris and Brussels and to drive all over Scotland. Our first year of parenthood unfolded idyllically, from the setting to the rhythm of life. Our jolly, curious little boy hit all of his physical milestones on time as he closed in on his first birthday. It was a happy and uncomplicated time for all three of us.

Paul's first year was what we had come to anticipate after reading books like the popular *What to Expect* series. Like most parents, we took for granted that Paul would be special in our eyes, but also just another typically-developing child. In the months following his first birthday, I threw away all of my child development books because none of them seemed to apply to our child anymore. The more time Paul and I spent with other toddlers in our building, the clearer it became that Paul was quite a bit quieter than his peers. Many of the other children were adding new words to their vocabulary weekly. Paul lagged behind, making sounds but not articulating any words at all. Not even Mama or Dada. I had concerns, but heard "let's wait and see."

When Paul was 16 months old, we said goodbye to London to move back to the US for my husband's new job. We left behind a tight community and a walk-everywhere city lifestyle. In the States, we moved into a suburban two-story house near a quiet wooded area and drove everywhere we went. The move was a big change for all of us, most of all Paul, who seemed to miss the comfort of his old London rhythms and routines. Anxiety set in for Paul, and he seemed to turn inward. While Paul and I were attuned enough to each other that daily life was smooth and predictable, he still had not yet spoken one word. Pointing and leading me by the hand were the communication methods Paul relied on.

When it was time for Paul's 18-month check-up at his new US pediatrician, there was much cause for concern. At the end of this appointment, his new pediatrician casually said she thought the speech delay might be related to autism, and there was not much that we could do at the moment. I was flooded with questions about our son and his future. Would Paul ever speak a word? Would he ever have a friend? Would he be able to have a job and live independently one day? Autism was occasionally reported in the news in 2002, but I didn't know of a single child with the diagnosis. I felt shattered leaving the appointment. Shattered and pregnant with our second child.

With another baby coming in a few months, there was an imperative to find answers and establish a plan while Paul was my one and only responsibility. We met with an experienced developmental pediatrician who was non-committal about a specific diagnosis, but reassured us that Paul would speak one day, which was tremendously reassuring. This doctor also had a relatively passive approach to intervention, which I couldn't accept. From the day after Paul's visit to Johns Hopkins to the birth of his younger brother a few months later, I relentlessly pursued early intervention resources and an inclusion model preschool for Paul.

I got a lot of practice being resourceful and politely assertive in the service of our son. Years later, a friend told me he referred to me as the velvet steam roller, and it's one of the most flattering things anyone has ever said to me. Even though Paul's struggles were not what I would have chosen for him or for our family, I was more at peace having a plan in place and working with the knowledgeable professionals on Paul's team. During this time, I came across a metaphor that helped shift my thinking. When you learn your child has a disability, it can feel like you've landed in Holland when you were expecting Spain. You grieve the trip you planned and the destination you were expecting while gradually discovering the unexpected beauty and lessons of the place where you've actually landed. Little by little, my grief abated, and I relaxed and started to appreciate Holland.

Here is what I never could have anticipated. What started out as a state of blinding panic evolved into a new mindset that touched all aspects of my life and has left me forever changed for the better. Until becoming a mother, I had enjoyed so much autonomy and control in all aspects of my life. One paradox I discovered early on is that tight control can be reassuring, but it's also exhausting. For the first time, I had no choice but to surrender and accept the circumstances that had shown up. I wasn't defeatist or resigned, but nor was I actively resisting reality. And in time, my attitude evolved from one of fear and victimhood to neutrality to a firm belief that there was a higher order at work. It dawned on me one day that I had chosen Paul, and he had chosen me. That belief about Paul and my two younger children changed everything. I was humbled and remain so by the valuable lessons and insights each of my three children has taught me.

Paul had the great fortune to attend a preschool where he received expert social-emotional instruction as well as speech and occupational therapy built into the school day. He had neurotypical and neurodiverse classmates. Getting to know the parents of the other special needs students who were navigating the same challenges was a huge relief from the isolation I felt. The school community was just the start of the snowball of people in my growing special needs Silver Linings community. There were parents, teachers, and therapists of all kinds who became important pillars in Paul's and my life. These are people I treasure and would never have met but for Paul and his early challenges. Before becoming a mother, I'd worked in the corporate world and did interesting work with smart, dynamic people. My job and professional relationships were satisfying on an intellectual level, but not deeply meaningful in the way motherhood and the heartfelt bonds shared in this special community are.

When I reflect back on who I might be, what I might value, and what my life might be like today had I not been fortunate enough to be Paul's mother, I'm confident it would lack the richness, the perspective, the compassion, and the depth that feel core to who I am. I mourn some aspects of the life that would've come with a neurotypical child, but in the end, I think I've gained much more than I've lost. Now that Paul is a happy and independent young man, I feel called to share a message of hope and empowerment with parents everywhere, whomever their child may be.

CHAPTER

Thirteen

Awakening the Courage to Change

Karen Ledwidge

Karen Ledwidge

Karen Ledwidge is a credentialled counsellor, mentor, meditation teacher, author, artist, intuitive and spirit medium offering her time and services to people worldwide. She lives on the west coast of British Columbia, Canada, with her family. Surrounded by the rugged beauty of Canada's ocean and forests, Karen spends most of her time immersed in nature. She is passionate about living spiritually, helping others heal and retreating with her family and closest friends to places that awaken her love of life and bring her joy. To find out more about Karen's services, contact her at www.insightswithkaren.com.

Chapter 13

Awakening The Courage to Change

By Karen Ledwidge

Standing in a whirlwind of my intense, tearful sadness, I felt pulled under into a deep sea of disbelief, confusion, and devastation. My life was collapsing around me. I had become used to his destructive emotional highs and lows and erratic behaviors. I had often tried to change him. For years, I lived in denial, trying to convince myself and others that it was not that bad. The addiction he suffered was destroying him, me, and our family. It was an emotional roller coaster that I needed to get off. But fear immobilized me.

My husband stood before me in his alcoholic madness. I stood motionless, my heart pounding in my chest. It was the first time I saw my life as it was. The fairy tale was over. The kind, intelligent and loving man I fell in love with years before was lost. He was engulfed in the raging storm of his addiction and chaos that crept into our lives through the years. At first quietly, as he hid the alcohol, debt, and lost work time. Slowly, he left us as he sank deeply into the abyss.

The escalating conflict was unbearable. The children were suffering. I endured what seemed like endless distress and sleepless nights for months on end. But somewhere deep inside me, I felt the strength and courage to keep going, for the children and me. I had to. He was lost to us. But I was not lost anymore. It was time to leave.

In the aftermath of the divorce and chaos that ensued, I was flooded with distress that intensified as the weeks went on. A mosaic of thoughts raced in all directions in my mind amidst scrambled emotions. Fear, anger, and sadness were overwhelming as I grieved the end of my marriage and began to gather up my life with forward motion and glimpses of hope. The beginning of imagining a better life. The way was long and arduous at times. The unbearable grief would subside and rest in some resolve until the next wave flooded in. I felt alone and isolated in my sorrow. But I knew I had to keep going not only for me, but for my children, who were more precious to me than life itself. They were surviving, too. We were striving and rising stronger together. I soothed my fear and found courage.

A spark of energy lit within me. Its vibrance coursed through every fibre of my being. It resonated like a beacon of light, clearing the way home for those lost at sea. I could see the devastation of our lives more clearly, and in those fleeting moments, I knew I could survive. In the depths of my being, I knew my strength and courage were there. It had to be. How else could I have come this far and survived so much turmoil, heartache, and loss? Memories of happier times that had faded in the background of my mind trickled in from time to time. I knew I needed to be happy again. This compelled me forward.

During the next several years, I dedicated myself to healing my mind, body, and spirit. I was recreating myself and my life. Nurturing, treasuring, and growing the good parts, purging the unhelpful parts, and creating the new parts of myself. I remembered the tough changes I had endeavoured and overcome. This encouraged me.

Hope danced in my wiser spiritual self. It was the place deep within me that felt connected to something greater than myself. An intelligent consciousness that was safe, warm, and loving. A source of my strength and courage. In those pivotal moments, I knew I was not alone. I was engulfed in a sense of peace and serenity that arose in me like a sunrise warming the earth and all its beings as it rises from its horizon across the ocean. I was on my way back to myself. I could feel my light and hope awakening.

Creating a new home for my children and me was paramount. My children needed and deserved a stable, healthy family and home. Fear and uncertainty of where we would live, the affordability and well-being of the children resolved. Our new home was a place of joy, comfort, calmness, and love. It took courage and strength to be a single parent, and sometimes I was afraid and stressed by all the changes and responsibilities. I learned to ask for help from kind, loving people who wanted to support me. Close family members, knowledgeable professionals, and support groups of people who had lived through similar experiences.

I faced the fact that I cannot control or fix others or their addictions. I continued to focus on myself, my needs and those of my children. I found purpose and meaning in my life. I dealt with the loss and grief of the marriage and earlier losses. I went to therapy, felt my feelings, learned about addiction in relationships and families, and healed my wounds. I learned new self-care strategies and skills, such as how to spend undistracted quality time with myself: meditating, nature walking, mindfulness, breathing techniques such as deep breathing, Vipassana and yoga breathing; positive self-talk, and creative expression such as writing for emotional healing. Interweaving self-compassion, self-love and self-respect was central to my healing and development and still is as I continue to meet challenges, grow and change.

I embraced my whole self, including the part of me that felt eternally connected to a magnificent conscious intelligence of the universe. This loving source became my refuge, healer, companion, and confidant. I read spiritual books from all faiths and philosophies. Compassion and meditation practices became an integral part of my daily life. I sought teachers and spiritual guides and attended meditation retreats. I discovered the expansiveness of myself that was awakened in childhood. Along the way, I found loving spiritual friends.

Helping people find their courage became a passion. I was driven to help those enduring lives of chaos and suffering. I eventually changed careers, returned to school, achieved two degrees, volunteered in my community, and immersed myself in a rewarding counselling career. Building strong and healthy relationships with myself and others became paramount. I came to know that the most important relationship I would ever have is the one I have with myself. This relationship is central to overall well-being and all other relationships. Developing this inner strength requires unconditional self-love, compassion and respect, knowledge, awareness of strengths, and coping abilities. All are essential for navigating through the sunny, rainy, snowy, and mountainous terrains of life. Seeking support from trusted family, friends, professionals and like-minded people nourished my need to belong, to be seen and heard, to be valued and loved unconditionally. Addiction in families is destructive, and I knew I did not want that. I increased my knowledge of what healthy relationships and families look like and feel like.

I now know that everything occurred with purpose, was timely and essential to becoming the person I am in a life filled with love, passion, hope, joy, and adventure. Fear, uncertainty, and a lack of courage sometimes surface, but I can work through it with self-confidence. Most fear is fueled by false thoughts that thrive with excess attention and future uncertainty. Fortunately, humans are naturally programmed to survive, adapt, overcome, and thrive. I am more courageous than I thought, and this is true for most people. With the help of special people along the way, I found the courage to change myself and my life. If you have lived or are living through the chaos of addiction or other hardship, as sure as you are reading this, you are already awakening your strength, courage, and hope!

Everything changes sooner or later. I have gained the wisdom to know the difference between what I can and cannot change and the courage to change what I need and can. Change can compel us forward and present opportunities for a better life and a stronger, happier self. I grew to love and respect myself and to exclude the people who do not. I came to know the power of compassion and forgiveness for myself and others. My former spouse, too, has courageously healed and grown, and we are now friends. Compassion heals, is gentle, peaceful and loving. Encourage yourself forward with self-compassion, use your own strategies and feel welcome to consider and use the ideas that I have shared. I hope you will feel inspired to face and ease your fears, know your strength and courage and free yourself from the situations that are stopping you from living the magnificent life you deserve.

CHAPTER

Fourteen

Standing at the Edge

Joe McMonagle

Joe McMonagle

Joe McMonagle is a spirit healer who uses storytelling to help people reconnect with their innate goodness, deepen their relationship with the divine, and discover healing and insight into their life's purpose. He holds degrees in Architectural Engineering (B.A.E.), Divinity (M.Div.), and Counseling Psychology (M.A.), reflecting a diverse background that grounds his spiritual and professional work.

Joe's journey started with 12 years in religious life, followed by 26 in the software industry. His spiritual fantasies, *Shadows and Light* and *Where the Heart Leads*, form the first two volumes of his five-book *Journeys of a Spirit Healer* series. His short story, "Not Yet Skyborne," set in the same world, is freely available on his website. Joe has also contributed chapters to *Awaken Your Magic: Real Life Manifestation Journeys*, *Guided By Spirit: A Quest for Self-Discovery, Insight & Illumination*, and *The Power of Vision: Inspiring Possibilities, Creating Change.* All were published by As You Wish Publishing.

Committed to ongoing personal and spiritual growth, Joe continues to study wide-ranging belief systems and healing practices with spiritual teachers, including Denise Linn, Terry Bowen, Valerie Jew, Dougall Fraser, Radleigh Valentine, Liz Dawn, and Kyle Gray. Visit www.joemcmonaglehsp.com to connect with Joe and explore his work.

CHAPTER 14

Standing at the Edge

BY JOE MCMONAGLE

"You've got to be kidding. You want me to leap that?"

Before me lay a dark chasm. I couldn't see its bottom; I could only sense that monsters lurked within. Should I take the risk? My gut said no. I was certain I would fall in and face endless torment.

You see, my storm took another shape. Though it wasn't real, the image formed in my mind after a question from the man sitting across from me, Justin Dyzkowicz.

Justin was a Benedictine monk whom I had asked to be my spiritual director. I was a novice in my first year of formation for the Catholic priesthood. The week before, my novice master had asked my novice mates and me to work with a spiritual director as we discerned our journey ahead.

Earlier in the meeting, I had shared my story with Justin, including my beliefs about God, myself, and my place in the world. During this time, he remained mostly silent, encouraging me to continue speaking about what brought me to this moment.

As I did, I wondered what he thought. Would my piety and my adherence to the Church's teachings impress him? Or would he reject me for the times I failed to follow them perfectly?

Understand that for the first 24 years of my life, leading up to this meeting, I thought there was something wrong with me. I was quiet and sensitive, and I wasn't interested in sports like other boys. I was also gay, which Catholicism deemed disordered. For someone raised to believe the Church held the truth, there was no room to question it. As a result, I buried my feelings so deeply that I forgot they existed.

I became an actor trying to portray the perfect, normal son, student, and Catholic. I desperately sought approval, not only from adults but from anyone, including children. To maintain this role, I carefully reviewed every decision before making it and never took risks. I was afraid that doing so would break my cover and make me stand out, revealing the worthless and disgusting me.

After finishing my story, convinced I had kept the real me hidden, Justin spoke, "Joe, you don't need a spiritual director. You need a therapist."

Oh, no. He's rejecting me, I concluded. He had figured out how awful I was. Two other thoughts quickly followed: He's going to tell my novice master. I'll be kicked out of the Paulist Fathers.

Before I could verbalize my fears, Justin added, "I'm a licensed therapist and will work with you if you wish. Would you consider that instead of spiritual direction?"

I gulped. "Do you truly understand what you're asking?"

I then described the terrifying chasm. I also explained how staying on this side, with my rules about what people and situations to avoid, kept me mostly safe. Even though I hadn't answered his question, I hoped sharing that was enough to make him reconsider.

It didn't. Justin said nothing.

My mind spun. How could I say yes to his invitation? Justin was asking me to let go of my protections, face my feelings, and the hidden childhood torments lurking in the deep. Why would I want to put myself through that?

Have you been in this situation? Maybe a therapist, a friend, or a family member encouraged you to share your deepest fears and pains. Though you knew you were barely getting by, you believed it would be far worse to face them. After all, wasn't it better to pretend and keep the peace at any price, especially if someone might accuse you of making it all up?

I know of some who have said yes to this question, and their lives appeared fine. Why shouldn't I do the same?

Yet something in me resisted the idea. Remembering why I was meeting with Justin, I asked him three questions: Wouldn't accepting his invitation mean that we'd be focusing on me and my needs? Aren't Catholics supposed to be selfless? And, as a priest, shouldn't my attention be on serving my parishioners and fulfilling their expectations, as I had done with others all my life?

Rather than answer, Justin asked another question: "Don't you think what you believe about yourself will affect how you minister?"

That stopped me cold.

I flashed back to my decision to become a priest. I was certain of my calling to serve. It came out of my desire to share the reality of a loving and compassionate God, so different from the judging and condemning one I grew up believing in. I also felt guided by God to this life, including to the Paulist Fathers. If jumping the chasm meant being able to do that, how could I say no?

But could I trust Justin with all my fears? Wouldn't I disgust him? And worse, by taking the leap and opening myself up, would he hurt me? People lie or use you for their purposes.

Despite those worries, I realized two things. First, my choice of Justin as a spiritual director was another example of God guiding me. What were the chances that the person I chose was a therapist, and that he suggested we set aside the original purpose of our sessions?

Second, Justin didn't use judgment or guilt to force me to agree. He had offered an invitation.

In my heart, despite the terror, I felt a spark of courage. Though small, it was enough.

Looking into Justin's compassionate eyes, I gave my answer: "Yes."

I would leap the chasm and face my deepest secrets, as long as he was there with me.

Justin assured me he would be. He further said that should a hidden monster or memory overwhelm me, we'd slow down, invite it to come forth so we might understand it and ease the pain.

Over the next ten months, we worked steadily. I shed many tears. I eventually felt lighter and began believing there was another way to live. I also considered the possibility that I was not as awful a person as I thought.

When I completed the novitiate and moved on to the seminary, my superiors encouraged me to continue the process with another therapist.

Since then, I've had other chasms to leap. None were as large as the one I described. But the success of my first leap with Justin gave me the courage to leap again.

As for what survived the storm, I didn't just survive. I was reborn. Over the ensuing years, I discovered the real me: the loving, worthy, and blessed me. That led me to leave the priesthood and follow a different path of service. I also came out publicly as gay and married a wonderful man.

I am forever grateful to Justin and the Paulist Fathers for giving me back to myself. Not only did this experience enable me to enjoy life, it helped me better serve others and encourage them to recognize their innate goodness as divine souls. I further realized that sharing how I faced my chasms and the terrors within was equally important. For in hearing my story, people might glimpse theirs and sense that healing is possible for them as well.

If you're standing at the edge of a dark and dangerous chasm, fearful of what you might find if you leap, seek someone you trust who will jump with you. Know that God and the angels stand at your side, offering their support and encouragement.

Then take the risk. You can do it. You are a powerful and courageous person, even if you don't feel like it at the moment. While it may be painful, the healing you experience will open you to the beautiful and holy you.

CHAPTER

A Hand in the Dark
John Mothershead

John Mothershead

John Mothershead (he/him) is an intuitive artist, angel coach, and creator of Color Your Spirit, Angel Party 365, and Angel Party Tarot, tools that help others align with creativity, ritual, and divine connection. With certifications in Reiki, angelic healing, and color coaching, John combines grounded wisdom with spiritual insight to help people reclaim their power and live in full color. He writes about survival, becoming, and the courage to stay, using his own story of navigating crisis and choosing life to help others find their way through the fog. When not creating, John still experiments in the kitchen, snuggles with his dogs, and volunteers in his community.

Content Note: This chapter references suicidal ideation and a suicide attempt. If you're in immediate danger, call your local emergency number or text 988. You don't have to carry this alone. More support and resources are available at johnmothershead.com/youarenotalone.

CHAPTER 15

A Hand in the Dark

BY JOHN MOTHERSHEAD

> "The sensitivity that makes you hurt this deeply will help you love fiercely, create beautifully, and see what others miss. Your pain is refining you, not ruining you."
>
> John Mothershead

Most weekends in high school, I had the house to myself. My parents drove inland to care for my grandmother as dementia carried her away. My sisters were gone, one at college, one in Mozambique with the Peace Corps.

Those days alone, I let my guard down.

I'd sprawl on the carpet with hand-me-down *Sports Illustrated* magazines, linger over photos of beefy Olympians like I was studying anatomy for a test. I'd climb onto the coffee table and belt show tunes at full volume, "La Vie Bohème" to an audience of nobody. I'd dial up the early internet and slip into AOL chat rooms, talking to strangers who would never know my face or my fear.

And because my mother was famously OCD-clean, I used my alone time to do the most rebellious thing imaginable: bake complicated recipes with too many steps and ingredients, making glorious messes. Bowls piled up. Flour dusted the counter. I tried, failed, and tried again. In those private hours, I wasn't careful or quiet or shrinking. I was a teenager with big music and big feelings, playful, ridiculous, fully alive.

But I kept those parts hidden.

Monday through Friday, I tried to disappear. I was painfully shy and painfully closeted, moving through school as if everyone could see right through me. In the bathroom, I'd been shoved into urinals, locked in stalls, laughed at like it was sport. So I managed myself strictly. My mannerisms. My voice. My posture. My joy.

Carrying a hidden life gets heavy. I daydreamed about brighter days, a version of life where I could stop performing "normal," where I could be seen without being punished. I could imagine that future, but I couldn't grasp it.

And when the future feels like it's behind glass, darkness starts to feel like the only thing you can hold onto.

One weekend, I decided to bake cinnamon braided bread, the kind that belongs in bakery windows, glossy and golden, sugar tucked into every fold. This was before my mom's decades-long battle with ants, when I naively trusted myself to clean up the mess without her noticing.

The kitchen smelled like warm milk and yeast. I kneaded until the dough turned soft and elastic, and for a while, it soothed something in me. My hands doing something honest. My mind quieting.

Then it was time to shape it.

I rolled the dough out and began slicing long strips to braid. The knife moved with the ease you get from repetition, steady and predictable.

Slice. Slice. Slice.

It was a gentle meditation.

But somewhere between one cut and the next, my thoughts drifted.

Away from the bread.

Away from my presence.

To what it might feel like if the pain finally stopped.

It arrived like morning coastal fog, quiet, thick, inevitable. My mouth went dry. My body felt miles away. The world got strangely quiet, like someone had turned the volume down and left me alone with one sentence looping:

It's over.

The knife was in my hand. Heavy. Real.

I'll stop myself, because I want to be careful here. There is nothing romantic about a teenager reaching the edge. It was a kid who didn't know how to tell anyone he was drowning. It wasn't a plan or a poem. It was just unbearable.

And just as the knife moved from the dough to my skin—

Crash.

The mailbox slammed outside.

My body jerked like it had been awakened from a dream. The knife slipped from my grip and clattered to the floor.

The mailman.

I stood there stunned, staring at the knife as if it belonged to someone else. I could have stayed in that kitchen. I could have stepped back into the fog.

But I moved anyway, compelled by something I couldn't name.

I opened the front door and checked the mailbox.

Inside was a single envelope with my name on it.

My sister's handwriting.

Even now, I can picture it. Her perfect, rounded letters. The kind that looked a little like mine, but cleaner and steadier. The loops were deliberate. The lines even. My name written like it mattered.

A letter from Mozambique.

I can't tell you what it said. I saved plenty of things at that age, ticket stubs, photos of crushes, entire grudges, but not the one piece of paper that arrived like a hand in the dark. I wish I had it now, if only to remember exactly how she did it.

But I remember what it did.

I remember tearing it open with shaking hands and reading it right there in the doorway, sunlight on the floor behind me, kitchen darkness at my back. The paper was thin and worn, as if it had traveled across the world to find me. My throat tightened. My eyes burned.

Her handwriting offered something I couldn't find on my own: knowing my sister, she'd written paragraphs, maybe pages. But what I heard through all of it was:

I see you.

I fell down and sobbed, messy, body-shaking tears. The kind of crying that happens when your nervous system finally stops pretending you can carry it all alone.

When I could breathe again, I went back to the kitchen. The knife on the floor, the dough on the counter, the cinnamon in need of sprinkling.

I picked up the knife.

Just a tool.

I finished slicing the dough. I braided it slowly, intentionally. I sprinkled cinnamon and sugar into the folds.

The hum of the refrigerator sounded like an accusation.

I kept going.

That was the miracle. Not sudden happiness or instant transformation. Just a choice. One small, trembling, ordinary choice to make it through the next hour.

That letter didn't fix everything. I still had hard days. I still had moments when the fog crept back in. But it gave me something I didn't have before.

Permission to stay.

Not because I was suddenly better, because I wasn't. Because I was still becoming.

Letter to the Reader

If the weight feels unbearable, if your mind is telling you you don't belong here, let this be your interruption, the way that envelope was mine.

Maybe you don't have a sister in Mozambique. Maybe you don't have someone who knows what to say. Maybe you don't even have words for what you're carrying.

But you have this page.

Here is the letter I wish someone had handed me sooner:

You are seen, even when you feel invisible.

You don't have to earn your place here. You already belong because you exist. The world needs your particular heart, your vision, the gifts only you carry.

The pain you're in doesn't mean you're broken. It means you've been becoming something the world isn't ready to hold yet. The sensitivity that makes you hurt this deeply will help you love fiercely, create beautifully, see what others miss. Your pain is refining you, not ruining you.

This darkness isn't the end of your story—it's the middle. And the middle is always hardest. But people are waiting to meet the you that comes after this. The you who bloomed through concrete.

You don't have to worry about tomorrow or even today. Just the next hour. That's all you need to hold right now.

Stay for the smallest things: a favorite song, warm bread, light on a wall. Stay for people who will love you exactly as you are. Stay because your story isn't finished and the world needs you in it.

If you need help staying, reach for it now. Call someone. Text the number below. Let someone stand with you. Asking for help isn't weakness; it's how we survive the unsurvivable.

When the fog rolls in, come back to your body. Find one anchor. Choose the next hour. You've survived every hard moment so far. You can survive this one, too.

And one day, you'll look back at this moment and realize: the pain that almost ended you became the foundation of everything beautiful you built after.

A Ten-Minute Return

Name one true thing. "Right now, I feel ___." No fixing. Just naming.

Choose one anchor. Water. Feet on the floor. One minute outside. A hand on your heart.

Write one sentence you need to hear. "I am allowed to ___." "I can make it through ___." "I don't have to do this alone."

Take one next step. Text someone you trust. Ask for help. Schedule support. If you are in immediate danger, call your local emergency number. In the U.S., call or text 988.

Hope isn't a floodlight. It's a flicker. Small, steady, and enough to lead you out of the dark.

CHAPTER *Sixteen*

In the Eye of the Storm
Deborah Rahalski

Deborah Rahalski

Deborah Rahalski is a cosmic adventurer who has been fascinated by the universe since childhood. She brings the same curiosity and wonder to her work as an astrologer and angelic energy artist. Her goal is to be a compassionate catalyst for change as she helps people find practical solutions while navigating the challenges of this human experience. Deborah bases her work on the belief that each of us consciously chooses the moment we arrive to begin our current life's journey. That moment becomes a sacred contract between our souls and the divine universe, so each person's natal chart represents the unique energies encoded in that moment. Deborah believes casting a chart creates a cosmic map that reveals possibilities rather than predictions. Her goal is to cut through complex astro-speak and guide her clients to a clear understanding of their inherent strengths and potential for growth and the fulfillment they came here to experience.

She invites you to embrace the cosmic adventure of finding her here by exploring more at www.deborahrahalski.com

Chapter 16

In the Eye of the Storm

By Deborah Rahalski

When I received the invitation to write a chapter for this book, I hesitated to accept.

The hesitation was not from doubting my capacity to write. This book is my fifth collaboration with this publishing family, and all four previous projects have been successful. If I was not hesitating from fear of writer's block or concerns about how this project would be supported, why did I almost decline the invitation? At the time the offer came, I was in the midst of a situation very much like a storm, and it was clear the situation would not be resolved before the book deadline. Yet there was something about the invitation arriving right after an intense round of prayers and meditation that felt like a response. It was one of those moments when I felt an intangible connection to a spark of hope. It's a subtle form of synchronicity easy to miss when navigating a stormy situation.

Recognizing synchronicity plays a major role in how I navigate life. Learning to trust those moments is a skill that helps me meet challenges. The louder the storm, the more essential trust in my internal GPS becomes. So, taking a few deep breaths to still the voice of doubt trying to stop me, I clicked the link to register. Then I went for a walk to settle the ripples of panic.

"What were you thinking? You do not have the time or energy for this project, not with all the chaos and confusion happening in our life! The last thing you need right now is the pressure of another deadline."

I let the voice ramble as I walked. All that mattered was that the offer felt like the light at the end of a long, dark tunnel, and I intended to follow it.

Soon after I received confirmation of our project, I noticed the submission date had been pushed forward several weeks. The new timeline was a relief and a clear message. Even as the dynamics of what was happening around me intensified, it felt like a validation of my choice. It would all become fuel for writing about surviving the storms of life. As plot twists morphed into revelations, I began to laugh at how it was all playing out. "Oh, so you want to write about surviving storms? Here are some fresh new ways to experience that. Take notes."

Notation number one: There is truth and wisdom in the adage, "Be careful what you ask for."

Notation number two: Having a sense of humor helps.

As I am well into my seventh decade of the adventure of being human, there have been a great variety of storms during my journey. From the time I was born until I headed off to college, my family moved eight times, and we lived in five different countries. The constant change taught me to meet uncertainty with curiosity. There have been earth and human storms, including an F4 tornado, typhoons and hurricanes, political unrest and martial law, date rape, the stillbirth of a child, a miscarriage and raising two brilliant, fiercely independent daughters. I am most proud of that last one, so for any of you who are raising kids, hang in there. We do the best we can, and if you let your heart lead the way, you'll all grow through the storms together.

That right there is the heart of what life's challenges have taught me: no matter what a storm takes from us, finding the will to rise from the losses matters because who we become as we rise is our gift to ourselves and to this world. When our first child, a son we named Zachary Thomas, was stillborn, my grief brought pain so deep I did not think I would survive. Seven weeks before my due date, we discovered that Zach had serious developmental anomalies, caused by a random genetic mutation known as trisomy 18. We left the doctor's office reeling from the shock. The next day, I went into spontaneous labor, and that devastating diagnosis became a blessing as it ensured no extraordinary measures were taken to intervene when Zach's heart stopped before delivery. As soon as I was stabilized in recovery, I asked to see him. The nurse went to find my attending physician, who explained what to expect. “I just need to hold him once so I can say goodbye,” I said.

When the nurse brought Zach in, he was wrapped in a blanket and had a little striped cap covering his head. His eyes were closed; he looked so peaceful. I reached into the blanket to find one tiny hand and just held it. Tears streamed down my face as I kissed his forehead. I did not want to let go of him. I wanted that moment to last forever so I could hold him forever. Knowing that was not possible, I took a deep breath and handed our son back to the nurse.

This happened 38 years ago, and here I am right back in that moment, tears streaming down my face as I feel the love that blessed me that day. I did not perceive it as a blessing then. For days, I dreaded going to sleep because I did not want to wake up to the irrevocable truth of being a mother whose child was gone. I cried myself to sleep, and in the morning, I would stay in bed until I stopped crying. Weeks passed this way, and then one morning, I woke from a dream that recalled the real typhoons that happened when we lived in the Philippines.

Hurricanes and typhoons are tropical cyclones that have a wall of wind and rain circulating around a center called the eye. No matter how fierce the wind and rain are in the walls swirling around it, the eye in the center is calm. When these storms make landfall, there is an onslaught of fierce winds and heavy rain as the leading-edge storm moves in. The same happens when the other side of the storm passes through. Yet, as the storm moves over land, any place directly below where the eye passes over will have a period of calm. The winds die down, the rain stops, and the sky clears. It was a memory of living this remarkable experience, which came back to me as a dream that morning. It was the moment that started my shift from devastating grief to quiet hope because I woke with one clear thought, "I need to stay in the eye of the storm."

Making a conscious commitment to seek that eye of calm as grief ran through me eventually helped me understand what my grief was telling me. Zachary Thomas had blessed me by opening a deep well of love and sharing that love was the best way for me to transform my grief into a superpower. As the love deep within me began to feel stronger than sorrow, it awakened a fierce determination to be a mother. That determination would manifest as both a major career change and, more soulfully, as our two wonderful daughters.

Rising out of grief was one of the hardest storms I have survived. The challenges in my life have become quests that require courage and a commitment to go deeper every time a new storm hits. To find the eye in each of life's storms requires a willingness to confront my deepest fears and face the shadow side of myself that those fears feed. Every storm creates uncertainty. Uncertainty requires me to relinquish control, and that requires me to trust and have faith. If my faith begins to waver, it's a clear sign to disengage from the turbulence of a situation and find my way back to that central eye of calm. I get there by sheltering somewhere quiet, ideally a physical location. For situations when I cannot physically relocate, the practice of breathwork is an essential tool in my survival kit. Having a sense of humor, as listed in notation number 2 above, is also useful when appropriate. Gratitude is another beneficial practice, and I don't mean the "be grateful you have mushy peas because some people in the world are starving" gratitude. Consistently pausing at random moments throughout the day and asking, "What am I grateful for right here in this moment?" has amplified my ability to feel grateful even when life gets challenging. Asking for help is another important practice, and it recently helped move the situation I have been in closer to resolution while allowing me to remain objectively in the eye of calm.

These practices are the foundation of how I not only survive storms, but they are also the way I dare to thrive because of them. Life has taught me that no matter what a storm takes from us, finding the will to rise from the losses matters because who we become as we rise is our gift to ourselves and to this world.

CHAPTER

Seventeen

Kill Me Now
Kyra Schaefer

Kyra Schaefer

Kyra Schaefer is the Co-Founder and CEO of As You Wish Publishing, the company she built with her husband, Todd, in 2017 to help everyday people share their stories with clarity, integrity, and heart. Through their signature publishing package, Kyra leads the production of both print and eBooks in a way that keeps authors empowered and in control of their work. As You Wish Publishing is proudly third-party vetted by the Alliance of Independent Authors, meeting the organization's rigorous standards that protect authors from predatory or misleading publishing practices.

The books produced through As You Wish Publishing span personal growth, healing journeys, holistic business, spirituality, coaching, fiction, and more. Kyra and Todd have collaborated with hundreds of writers of all ages and backgrounds, celebrating a wide range of voices, styles, and creative expressions.

Kyra is also a bestselling author, known for *Writing with the Archetypes* and *Holograms and Echoes*. She creates workshops that blend insight, creativity, and play, offering small groups a grounded and meaningful space to explore their stories. Her background includes certifications in Positive Psychology, Art Therapy, and advanced training in Neurolinguistics and Hypnosis. For more than twenty years, she has supported thousands of clients through her work as an emotional healing practitioner. Find her at www.asyouwishpublishing.com.

Chapter 17

Kill Me Now

By Kyra Schaefer

At 22 years old, it seemed that everything was set. I had a job I could stay in for 30 years and a mortgaged home that I loved. Three bedrooms, two baths, plenty of room for my dog and two cats, big beautiful trees, and a landscaped yard I had planted and cultivated with my own hands. The only problem with all of this: I wasn't emotionally well.

I was addicted to alcohol and cigarettes. I was overweight and unhealthy, both mentally and physically. You would think a person with such a lovely setup couldn't possibly be so miserable. But I was, and the people in my life reflected that back to me.

I naturally orbited mostly addicted individuals. How could I possibly be around people who were healthier than I was? How could I stand to be judged by people who seemed to have their lives together? No. I needed people who would support my painful lifestyle. I needed to be swallowed up by my anxiety and pain and just sit in it. I needed to keep supporting a fiancé whose moods I tracked the way you track weather, by small signs before the storm, and by how many beers were left in the fridge.

Until I met her.

There are moments in our lives that define us. I can clearly see that this moment changed me forever. I walked into a metaphysical store in Richmond, Virginia, with a friend of mine. Out of the back room walked a woman who, when I saw her, fixed something inside me. I was in awe; she was radiant. When she spoke, there was a deep knowing. "Hello, how can I help?" I turned away to catch my breath. "I'm okay," I said, clearly, not okay. "Let me know if you need anything," she affirmed, with a bounce in her voice.

Let her know if I needed anything? Really, anything? How about an energetic, physical, emotional, and mental overhaul? Because up until this moment, I hadn't realized that I had been missing something vital. Something pure, true, and harmonious. She unlocked something in me, and she had no idea that she would be a catalyst for the most transformative moment of my life.

Within a few weeks, I visited the store again and learned that she was a Reiki teacher. She had struggled with alcoholism and had been through horrible situations that caused her to seek a better life with purpose and clarity.

I saw in her what I could become: healthy, whole, able, complete.

Things started to change in me. I wanted to go back to school, but my fiancé decided that was a ridiculous idea. How was I supposed to have his children and meet his needs if I was going to school? It was clear that paying for tuition was going to cut into his drinking fund, and this upset him terribly. I applied anyway and got accepted. He was not pleased.

All the while, I kept going to the metaphysical store and talking with this woman who was helping me see that a better life was possible. We never talked about my fiancé. We chatted about how energy flows through the body, chakras, and meditation. I started reading books, but I didn't want to share this part of myself with him. It felt too sacred and fragile. I was afraid that anything could shatter this newfound awareness if I shared it too soon. Instead, I started clearing the energy in my home. The first time I did a major clearing, everything changed.

I've told this story over and over, to police, lawyers, witness protection, judges, partners, survivors, clients, and teachers. The one thing that has always been consistent is that the story never changed. That's what trauma does sometimes: everything stays vivid and relivable for decades.

One crisp fall day, I cleared the energy in my home. I saged, burned candles, sprinkled salt water, and moved counterclockwise, starting upstairs and working my way down. I focused on the inside of the house and opened all the windows, calling for only positive energy to remain and asking that anything of a negative nature stay outside.

At that point, I hadn't stopped drinking. I had a couple of beers in me when I took my fiancé to a party out in the country. Toward the end of the night, he was already far gone, and I wanted to go home. He fell asleep on the ride back. He woke up in a full-on rage, wanting more alcohol and furious that I wasn't giving in to his demands. He hit me so hard he broke my glasses and knocked me to the ground, then repeatedly kicked me in the head and hurled full beer cans at me while I lay curled up on my porch.

So there I was, on the ground. And that's when it happened.

I hadn't prayed to God since I was a child. I figured I'd been abandoned, and since I had very few expectations that anyone would show up for me, I assumed God had better things to do.

I was eerily calm. I felt no pain, though I should have. I was badly bruised with multiple head injuries. My fiancé walked inside, seemingly finished with brutalizing me. I rolled onto my back and closed my eyes. I started to talk to God.

"If you want me to live, let me live. If not, let him kill me now. If you let me live, I will do my best to be of service."

Instantly, I felt a surge of love and a deep knowing: it will all be okay. I sat up with an energy I had never felt before.

I walked into the house, picked up the landline, dialed 911, and calmly told them there had been a domestic disturbance at my home. My fiancé then head-butted me and left. I wouldn't see him again until we were in court. He remembered nothing of the incident.

I wish I could tell you that this was the first time he had done something like this to me, but it most certainly was the last. I got the opportunity to decide his fate. I could send him to jail, or I could make him take anger management classes, go to AA, and complete a variety of other extremely annoying things he would hate. If he missed a single class, he would go directly to jail. Hey, I may have gotten a little enlightened, but even masters are insufferable at times.

I tried to find the woman who had started the change in me, who had fixed me simply by walking into a room. She had already resigned at the metaphysical store, but I needed real healing now, and I was finally ready. I had stopped drinking, and I needed the next step because, regardless of whatever had awakened in me on that porch, I still needed to clear out all of the abuse, all of the pain I had ever experienced. Otherwise, I was in real danger of falling back into who I used to be. I refused to go back. But I couldn't do it alone. I made a promise, not just to God, but to myself.

I found her. She had opened a healing center. That space would shape the next year of my life: personal healing, transformation, and learning what I was actually made of. What I didn't expect was that this time would also set into motion the next 25 years of my life, all the way to this moment, right now, writing this to you.

You may not see it, but the rooms you walk into change simply by your presence. Someone lost, alone, and afraid is watching you right now, the way I once watched a woman walk out of a back room and fix something broken in me without saying a word. You don't need to know their name. You don't need to know what you did. Just keep being your most loving self. That is the whole assignment. That is how healing echoes through all time and space.

I kept a promise made on a cold porch to a God I wasn't sure was listening. I got up. That's all it ever takes, just getting up one more time than you fall. If you are reading this, something in you is already getting up. Honor that. The chain reaction has already begun.

CHAPTER

Eighteen

Letting Go of Friendships

YuSon Shin

YuSon Shin

YuSon Shin is a gifted healer, intuitive, medium, speaker, author, and teacher of the healing and intuitive arts based in Los Angeles. She blends ancient wisdom with modern energy techniques to help people and pets heal physically, emotionally, and spiritually. With her joyful and compassionate approach, she empowers others to unlock their innate healing abilities and step into their full potential.

Passionate about teaching, she leads workshops to help students awaken their spiritual gifts, heal deep-rooted wounds, release energetic blocks, and create lasting transformation. She believes that healing is not a one-size-fits-all process and incorporates a wide range of modalities to meet the unique needs of each individual.

YuSon's expertise spans a vast range of healing modalities, recognizing that there is no "one-size-fits-all" approach to healing. She utilizes Akashic Records and Chinese energy healing techniques for past life, karma, and ancestral clearings. She is also an authorized practitioner of the Bengston Energy Healing Method, the only method scientifically proven to cure cancer. A certified Reiki Master, she also integrates Quantum Touch, Integrated Energy Therapy (IET), 5th Dimensional Quantum Healing, DNA Theta, and Access Bars. She is the author of eleven collaborative books, including *Holistic, Manifestations, Whispers From The Heart, Soul Warrior, The Empath Effect, Be Bold, Ignite Your Inner Fire, Awaken Your Magic: Real Life Manifestation Stories, Paws and Purpose, From Start-Up to Stand Out, The Resilient Heart* and *What Survives The Storm.*

You can reach YuSon at YuSon@ShinHealingArts.com and www.ShinHealingArts.com.

Chapter 18

Letting Go of Friendships

By YuSon Shin

When I look back on the most painful times of my life, the vast majority of them revolve around breakdowns with friends. Friends are often described as the family you choose, and because of that, we tend to enter friendships without expecting an ending. There is a saying that people come into your life for a reason, a season, or a lifetime. My heart wants to keep people close forever, and it struggles when those durations fall short. Although I am blessed with core ride-or-die friends, I still feel profound sadness when even peripheral friendships end. Unlike romantic relationships or family estrangements, there is no clear societal framework for friendship closure. This ambiguity leaves people vulnerable to confusion, anger, guilt, judgment, grief, maybe relief and a range of other emotions that are hard to reconcile.

Socializing is a fundamental human need. When you are surrounded by the right people, their company feels energizing rather than draining, while the absence of meaningful interaction can be deeply damaging; solitary confinement is considered a form of torture precisely because humans are not meant to exist in isolation. Genuine friendships nourish the soul, acting as safety nets that support us during moments of success and catch us when we feel like we are falling. Friends come to know us, understand us, and accept us anyway. We turn to friendships for validation, emotional support, laughter, shared experiences, solidarity, and psychological safety, investing significant time and emotional energy into maintaining these bonds. Because of that investment and inherent value, the deepest disappointments often occur when friendships—relationships we consciously choose—come to an end.

Research consistently shows that friendships are among the strongest predictors of happiness and longevity. Loneliness and social isolation are associated with a significantly increased risk of premature death. The World Health Organization reports that loneliness affects roughly one in six people worldwide and is linked to hundreds of thousands of deaths annually. Humans cannot thrive alone. The phrase "it takes a village" is often applied to raising children, but it equally applies to sustaining adult well-being. Many people long to find their tribe, soul family or chosen family—a group where authenticity is welcomed and reciprocity exists without judgment. To feel seen, understood, and valued creates a sense of belonging that anchors us to the world. In many ways, friendships function as social currency, affirming that our lives matter within a shared human network.

Friendships tend to form more easily when we are young because proximity and routine bring people together through school, activities, or early careers. In adulthood, that structure erodes. Life transitions reshape priorities and demand intentional effort to maintain connection. I have experienced friendship attrition as friends married and began spending more time with other couples. Later, children shifted their schedules and social circles again. Some friendships faded as people cared for aging parents, while others dissolved when friends moved across the country in pursuit of opportunity or lifestyle changes. These reasons are easier to accept because they are understandable and often beneficial for the other person, even when the distance hurts. Promises to stay in touch are sincere in the moment, yet conversations gradually become less frequent until silence replaces familiarity.

Research supports the idea that friendship turnover is normal. Sociologist Gerald Mollenhorst found that people replace roughly half of their close social connections every seven years, largely due to changing circumstances rather than conflict. While individual friendships shift, the overall number of relationships people maintain tends to remain stable, suggesting that new friendships emerge to match evolving life stages. Understanding this helped me reframe loss—not as personal failure, but as a natural rhythm of social life. Still, many people today feel their circles shrinking and making new friends is increasingly difficult.

The world changed dramatically after the COVID-19 pandemic, which altered social patterns in ways research is still catching up to measure. Many adults report increased loneliness since the pandemic. In my observation, prolonged isolation weakened social skills, with Zoom calls and social media serving as substitutes for connection. Communication has also become more abbreviated. Conversations that once unfolded through long phone calls or thoughtful messages now often consist of short texts or even emojis. While efficient, these exchanges can lack emotional depth. Mental health challenges intensified during this period, highlighting how essential meaningful friendships and community truly are.

The pandemic also reshaped public behavior. Increased anxiety, agitation, and social tension became more visible, often manifesting as rudeness, aggression, or impatience in everyday interactions. Reports of disruptive airline passengers rose sharply compared to pre-pandemic norms, while children born or raised during lockdown experienced delays in social development. Because people are typically on their best behavior in public, even more extreme struggles emerged behind closed doors, reflected in a significant rise in domestic violence. Friendships were strained by isolation, relocation, fears about physical safety and health, financial uncertainty, job insecurity, and increased personal responsibilities. The pandemic likely acted as a stress test for friendships and exposed relational weaknesses that already existed.

Sometimes, we need to intentionally step back from friendships. Common reasons include:

1. Limited time and emotional bandwidth. Life responsibilities may leave little room to nurture certain relationships or extra responsibilities. Honesty about your limitations allows friendships to shift naturally into lighter connections or acquaintanceships.

2. Lack of depth. Frequent interaction does not automatically equal intimacy. When meaningful sharing disappears, the relationship may no longer meet the definition of friendship.

3. Inauthenticity. A healthy friendship allows vulnerability and self-expression. If you cannot be yourself, emotional safety is missing.

4. Unreliability. You cannot count on them. Consistently failing to show up erodes trust, one of the core foundations of friendship. If this is a regular occurrence, this is a red flag.

5. Unhealthy dynamics. Disrespect, belittling, jealousy, competitiveness, manipulation, controlling, boundary violations and sharing your personal information outside of your circle are all violations of trust. When a friendship becomes one-sided or revolves around constant drama, trust begins to erode. Healthy friendships require mutual

effort—support, appreciation, and intentional nurturing from both people. Backhanded compliments, being used, controlling or sabotaging behaviors, or a lack of genuine happiness for your success are warning signs that the relationship may no longer be healthy. Boundaries are not selfish; they create safety and strengthen relationships when respected. At the same time, over-giving, over-functioning, and overextending yourself can signal fear disguised as kindness.

I learned this through a friendship with an empathetic narcissist that initially felt deeply affirming but later proved emotionally draining. The connection began with intense enthusiasm—what I now recognize as "friendship bombing," similar to love bombing in romantic relationships. Despite appearing empathetic, this person consistently left me feeling exhausted. Eventually, I realized that emotional depletion was information. Some people repeatedly cross boundaries or refuse accountability. In those cases, distance becomes an act of self-respect. Not everyone deserves unlimited access to your energy. If it is difficult to identify unhealthy dynamics, look instead for healthy markers: respect, reciprocity, honesty, active listening, compassion, generosity, and trust. A good friendship should leave you feeling safe, valued, and energized and allow you to be fully yourself.

6. Lack of enjoyment. You no longer enjoy your interactions. You don't like who you are when you are together. You no longer have anything in common.

Values, beliefs, interests or lifestyles are no longer aligned.

Perhaps the most confusing experience occurs when a friend ends the relationship without explanation. The lack of closure can feel especially painful because humans are wired to avoid social rejection. Losing a friendship activates grief responses similar to those experienced after death or divorce. You may question your worth, replay conversations, or search for meaning where none is offered. The absence left behind can feel like a hole in your emotional safety net.

Yet friendship loss is universal. Experiencing it does not mean something is wrong with you. Relationships are living systems that evolve as people grow, and not all growth occurs in the same direction. Grief is evidence that the connection mattered. Allow yourself to feel the full range of emotions—sadness, anger, nostalgia, even relief—without judgment. Each feeling acknowledges that something meaningful once existed.

Over time, acceptance emerges. You can appreciate the shared history and affection without needing permanent access to the person. Some relationships are transformative precisely because they shape who you become, teach boundaries, reveal values, or guide you toward deeper self-understanding. Closure does not always come from explanation; sometimes it comes from acceptance.

Friendships, like seasons, change whether we are ready or not. Growth often requires release. Holding onto people too tightly can prevent both individuals from evolving into the lives they are meant to live. Letting go does not erase love or invalidate the past. No matter who lets go first, the healthiest path forward is to release the relationship with gratitude. Accept change. Allow growth. Carry forward what was learned. And when friendships expire, let them end with love.

CHAPTER

Ninteen

The Freedoms My Mother Never Had

Janet Zavala

Janet Zavala

Janet Zavala is a certified coach, workshop facilitator, and bestselling author with over 35 years of experience in the corporate environment, including 15 years dedicated to coaching individuals and groups.

A bestselling author, Janet's first solo book, *The Nature of Transformation*, along with her contributions to multiple compilation books, has captivated readers and received critical acclaim.

Driven by a deep passion for empowering professional women and those navigating midlife transitions, Janet specializes in helping individuals cultivate confidence, release limiting beliefs, and embrace their innate strengths to reach new heights of success. Her work guides readers and clients in creating authentic, balanced, and fulfilling lives aligned with their aspirations and values.

Connect with Janet:

- Website: JanetZavalaCoaching.com
- Email: Janet@JanetZavalaCoaching.com
- Substack: Janet the Midlife Feminist @midlifefeminist

Chapter 19

The Freedoms My Mother Never Had

By Janet Zavala

I'm in the era of my life where I can look back and reinterpret my experiences. My lens is no longer solely focused on the trauma I went through. This new appreciation reveals what life must have been like for my mother. I was often the closest witness to the painful aftermath of the storms she survived with no support or guidance. For many decades, I was unforgiving about the choices she made. During my storms, I had shelter when she did not. I had options she didn't. I believe if she had access to the rights women of my generation had, she would have been less angry. Maybe she would have been happier.

Maybe she would have been a better woman.

A better mom.

My mom straddled an era of pre-women's rights and the 1960s and 1970s when women were fighting so hard for equality. She had four children under 10 when women were reading Ms. Magazine and struggling to get access to birth control.

Born in 1938, she leaned towards the pre-women's rights era where access and freedoms were limited, and women disappeared behind their husbands.

I straddled two eras too. Patriarchal messaging and conditioning flooded my home and the airwaves. I, however, lean more post-1970s women's rights. I didn't know a world without basic rights, even if equality, especially equal pay, was still a struggle. I knew no different.

Messages and Expectations

As a teen in the 1980s, I saw professional women in their business suits (picture business suits with white sneakers) hurriedly making their way to their offices. 1988's *Working Girl* showed smart, ambitious women in the workplace. Making a difference. Being respected for their ideas. It offered an alternative to the typical dutiful wife trope or MTV vixen images of women.

I had peak exposure to the "Oprah era." For all its faults, exploitation, wacky theories and platforming dangerous men, *The Oprah Winfrey Show* allowed women an opportunity to go inward. It showed us on a large scale how people are impacted by trauma. It showed us how we created coping strategies and how past trauma keeps showing up in destructive ways. Most importantly, it gave a pathway that we could heal and make our lives better, fulfilling and more joyful.

We found community, even from a distance. We found others who went through the same grief, explored new ideas, and celebrated bright, successful women. Together.

My mom didn't have access to this language or resources. But I did. I saw models of what you could become: a full woman, with talents and gifts to be utilized, not wasted. It felt like an opportunity where little pieces of your authentic self could be seen and appreciated. Pieces of you that never saw the light of day and surprised you.

These revelations, combined with no concept of what life would be like without this knowledge, freedom, and opportunities, opened doors in my mind to dream about my best life.

Education Era

My mom didn't get her high school diploma. She likely fled circumstances that made schooling difficult. Employment opportunities for educated women were limited. Diplomas and degrees were not needed to be a housewife. Consequently, I wasn't encouraged to get good grades or go to college.

After landing in a corporate job, my real education began. My previously unrecognized talents emerged. I saw the value of career success. I took advantage of all new opportunities to learn, grow and flex my skills. It gave me confidence and economic freedom. It opened space in my imagination of what was possible. It introduced me to mentors and women who inspired me.

My mom couldn't tap into any of this, through circumstance or choice. Her jobs consisted of low-paying retail work, while economic power was always held in the hands of the man she was with.

Marriage Era

My mom was 21 when she married my 32-year-old dad. In less than 10 years she had four kids. She carried with her childhood trauma, as we all do. Her generation carried trauma without the language to understand it. It was carried alone. No help or support. A woman's depression or anxiety became a personal failing instead of what it was, the result of abuse, neglect, or an inability to live in her truth.

These conditions turn you into someone looking for an escape. An escape from the pain. An escape from a life that leaves your life circumstances or choices up to a man. My mom had few economic options. I would be six (in 1974) by the time she got financial autonomy. Legislation was required to allow a woman basic rights of survival.

I was 23 when I had my son and got married two years later. The modern middle class requires a two-income household. I never considered not going back to work after my son was born. It was both a desire and a necessity, however it was still a choice. I had the option to continue working. It was an option that allowed me to make my own money and progress in my career.

My mom's only choice was to be a stay-at-home mom, which is not a choice when it's the only option.

Establishing my own relationship dynamics was influenced by how I saw my mom behave during her relationships. I mentally added to the list of things I didn't want to experience.

I didn't want to abandon myself to the point of being on the edge of mental illness. A place where you feel like you're drowning, and no one is coming to save you. If required, I could save myself.

I didn't want to lose myself in a man's name as if to show ownership. She would address herself as Mrs. "the man's first and last name." Her identity erased.

I didn't want to serve without also equally receiving. My mom would clear my stepdad's plate, when the sink was inches away from the table. I never saw reciprocation.

My dad praised me for serving my husband during a visit. It was a prideful WWII era and 1950s expression of my servitude. My mini-feminist self explained gently that my husband serves me at his family home. I don't serve him. We serve each other.

My mom had three children before my arrival. I stopped at one child. When marriages teeter on the edge of survival, having more children makes your finances and choices more complicated and difficult to execute.

Divorce Era

In 1974, my mom was 36 when she decided to divorce. No-fault divorce was available in California in 1969. Access to banking and financial autonomy was accessible to her when she started the process. Without those two critical rights, she would have had no options.

However, my mom was still steeped in the patriarchy and bound by her lack of education and restricted economic opportunities. As had become her pattern, she looked for a man to save her from situations she felt she couldn't otherwise extract herself from.

When I made the decision to divorce, I had assets I could rely on like my college degree and career success. Divorce is never easy. There were emotional, societal and economic challenges. But they were challenges I could solve for.

One of my motivations to divorce was to be the best and most healed human I could be, for my son and myself. I didn't want him to have a miserable, sad, angry, and dependent mother.

I wanted to be:

A whole mother.

A better mom.

A better woman.

My mom's motivation was survival. Mine was a legacy of independence and fulfillment. A life I hoped my son could model.

Midlife Era

During our midlife eras our lives diverged completely. My mom took the only road available to her where I paved my own.

She continued to rely on support and validation from men. She made choices to "stick it out" for the sake of survival where I could not settle for just surviving.

After her husband passed, she relied on her brother for housing and support. Then she relied on my brother, her only son, until her passing.

Our sons (and daughters) inherit a world shaped by the choices we had. And the choices we didn't have.

I built a small life that I made sure I could maintain independently. The quality of my life is not dependent on an economic situation that I, in most cases, cannot solve myself. My survival is not dependent on the precarious availability of someone else to save me. Community and support are necessary. Total dependence is frightening.

I stepped into midlife embracing all the wisdom I've gathered. All the knowledge and lessons. And all the friendships.

I welcomed the privilege and opportunity to evolve. I stepped into my feminist era with the conviction of someone who witnessed firsthand what the lack of opportunity and equality does to a woman.

Women are better people when we can make decisions about our own lives.

Women who are unable to make their own decisions about their body, marriage, divorce, finances, as well as having the ability to leave toxic situations are an ominous presence in the lives of others. Her pain will radiate to those within her proximity.

Looking Back with Clarity

In the near decade since my mom's passing, I look back objectively, not with complex emotions or longing for the type of mother that society and circumstances wouldn't allow. I can't ask her questions about facts or feelings now. I'm not confident she would have the emotional strength or language for that talk.

The one thing I can do now is offer her grace and understanding. I can offer my perspective into the good versus bad woman trope. I can speak to the binary definitions that are placed on women and the punishment they experience when judged too harshly. I can talk about the choices she must make, when only given options that aren't in her best interest. I can write with caution about what a future without the freedom I had looks like.

I can evaluate my mom's actions, whether they harmed herself or her children, through a lens of what society would have allowed women to do at those critical times in her life versus mine.

Mostly, I have the opportunity and responsibility to demonstrate the potential for all of us to be better women when we have choices and freedoms.

My mother lived in a world without choices. I lived in a world with choices. I evolved because I was allowed to. She survived because she had to. And now we are watching people try to drag us back to my mother's world. A world where women exist, mired in trauma, conditioned to be trapped in survival mode instead of enjoying the autonomy every human should have access to.

Being a better woman, better mom, better human requires freedom, access and equality. Without these things, a woman's quality of life diminishes significantly. Suicide rates rise. Domestic violence increases. Maternal mortality rates go up.

We deserve to be better women, not because we are better than our mothers, but because we have the freedoms they never did. We owe access to those same freedoms to our children, especially our daughters and granddaughters.

Truth Through Generations

Through my reflections, I've come to accept basic truths living as a woman, in all generations.

1. Women's rights hinge on a couple of key issues. One is financial autonomy. Women used to marry to be housed and fed. They were indentured. Make your own money. Never stop making your own money. Progressively make more if you can. Maintain your financial independence. If you share finances, have full access and be equally involved in decision making.

2. Make your own choices. Fall in love or don't. Get curious. Get married or stay single. Have kids or don't. Make big, scary choices in life. Experience bliss through fear and the unknown. Take chances and be cautious. You are multi-dimensional. Don't let anyone tell you who you are or what you should want.

3. Women were told for generations not to have dreams about their lives and careers. Have all the dreams. Big ones. Small ones. Making progress on your dreams kicks up the wind beneath your cape. It's fuel and energy. Harness it.

4. Women's rights, once thought of as irrevocable, cannot be something we lose focus on. We must be prepared to fight for our rights and the rights of every marginalized group.

Through the generations, our role as women has been the nurturers of our community. We must remember the threads that reach back and the threads that will go forward in time.

Survival shaped my mother. Choice shaped me. What shapes the next generation will depend on what we protect.

www.ingramcontent.com/pod-product-compliance
Lightning Source LLC
Chambersburg PA
CBHW051245050726
47594CB00001B/311

* 9 7 8 1 9 6 9 6 1 5 0 6 1 *